FLY

WITHOUT FEAR

Mary Warr

GROVE COTTAGE PRESS

GROVE COTTAGE PRESS
R.R. 1, Site 17, C-45
Gabriola Island, B.C. V0R 1X0

Canadian Cataloguing in Publication Data

Warr, Mary, 1937-
 Fly Without Fear

ISBN 0-9699506-1-6

Distributed by **Gordon Soules Book Publishers Ltd**. ● 1359 Ambleside Lane, West Vancouver, BC, Canada V7T 2Y9 ● PMB 620, 1916 Pike Place #12, Seattle, WA 98101-1097 US
E-mail: books@gordonsoules.com
Web site: http://www.gordonsoules.com
(604) 922 6588 Fax: (604) 688 5442

1.Fear of flying. I. Title
RC1090.W37 1998   616.85'225   C98-911028-1

Cover design by
Harry Bardal Design

Printed in Canada
by Hobby Printers
Nanaimo, B.C. V9V 1B7

To fearful flyers everywhere
and
to Ernie, my dear husband, very best friend
and travelling companion.

"You are the wind beneath my wings."

Henley and Silbar

Contents

ACKNOWLEDGEMENTS

Writing this book has certainly been a new and exciting experience for me. It has taught me the true meaning of patience. I have also come to realize how truly blessed I am to have so many supportive people in my corner. I would like to take a moment to thank all the people who have helped to make this book possible by sharing their knowledge and expertise with me and who made a gift of their valuable time.

To Captain Allan Snowie and Captain Murray Wright; Flight Attendants Roxanne Clark, RN. and Susan Bowerman; Brian Ireland, Superintendent of Security at Calgary International Airport; Gordon Lowe, Manager of Calgary Terminal Air Traffic Services Control Unit; George Cox, Air Traffic Services, Safety Operations, London, England; Phil Prudhomme, Maintenance Manager for Air Canada in Calgary; Corporate Travel Service Manager Leslie Muir; Joyce Jenkins, R.N., Wayne Jones, M.D. My appreciation to Air Canada and Canadian Airlines International for their co-operation and assistance. Thanks also to all my clients, who know what the fear of flying is all about. Your input is much appreciated. A very special thanks to my husband, Ernie, for the many hours of work he has done for me and for his love and support. And finally, to my editors, John Wilson and Susan Kerr, a big thank you for your patience. You truly are wizards of words and commas. Also to Brent Cooper for his expertise in layout and design. It would not have been possible without you.

To you all. My heartfelt thanks for your help and for believing in me.

PREFACE

The fear of flying was one of the most terrifying and debilitating experiences of my life. It came complete with full blown panic attacks, heart palpitations, nausea, shortness of breath and the certainty that I was about to die. The mere thought of boarding a plane could effectively ruin any excitement in holiday planning. Anxiety would start to build weeks before I had to fly and would continue after we had landed. It was just a matter of time before I had to reboard and fly home. How awful to have ruined another vacation worrying and hyperventilating needlessly.

Airplanes are scary. They defy logic, confine you, are uncomfortable, make strange noises and, most awful of all, they leave the ground while making even stranger movements.

The noises were terrifying and I couldn't get away from them. I was so afraid I was convinced that everyone was staring at me and that any second I would start shouting, "Let me out! Let me out!" That would really embarrass me in front of everyone.

Once I realized my uneasiness was because I was ill at ease in social situations and once I learned to identify the strange noises I was much calmer. Social fears were heightened by the unknown. While I may never be fully at ease flying, I am now confident that I can fly without all the anxiety and related problems. I can fly and enjoy myself too. How exciting and what freedom!

Patty K.
Calgary, Alberta

INTRODUCTION

I did not take my first flight until I was forty-two years old. The reason was, for many years I suffered from Agoraphobia. Agoraphobia is a fear of open spaces, of leaving one's security. By age forty-two, I was phobia-free, and ready to spread my wings.

It was an exciting time for us. My husband had been transferred from Toronto to Calgary and we were happy to be moving in a westerly direction. I was both thrilled and apprehensive about my first opportunity to fly. My husband was quite used to crossing the country on business, so I sat him down and had him describe, step by step, the flight process. He told me what to expect and when. It is always difficult to visualize something that you don't know or understand, but his careful descriptions helped me to prepare for that important first flight and to understand the complex procedures going on around me. However, all his work did not prepare me for the exhilerating speed with which the plane accelerated down the runway.

Despite my recovery from Agoraphobia, I still very much needed to feel in control. As the world sped by the window, I had a fleeting moment of complete terror. Were it possible I would gladly have stepped off of that plane. Fortunately, it was just a fleeting moment and once I remembered to relax, it went away. As soon as I had settled down, I truly enjoyed the new experience. Now, many years and thousands of air miles later, I am convinced that planes are the very best way to travel. Flying has opened up new doors for me, but that moment of terror has stayed in my memory. Now, when helping fearful flyers, I can understand the fear.

One of the great pleasures of my work as a Counsellor and Therapist is watching people learn to let go of their fears and to live normal lives. It is a delight to watch clients learn a new approach to flying that is less stressful and more enjoyable. A particular thrill is receiving postcards from far away places, bearing messages such as, "I made it" or "I can't believe I'm actually here," or best of all, "I enjoyed my flight."

I like to think of this book as an awareness handbook. Its aim is to help fearful flyers understand why they have their fear, restore their confidence and show them ways in which they can erase their fear and reduce their stress. I hope it will also encourage readers to approach flying with a more positive attitude and educate them in actual flight procedures. There is also a chapter for and about the partners of flight phobics, the invaluable support person.

My sincere hope is that, if you have a fear of flying, then this book will inspire you to begin eliminating your own fears so that you will be able to fly the friendly skies with peace of mind, joy in your heart and that you will in time, learn to love the freedom of being able to fly without fear..

PART ONE

The Problem

CHAPTER ONE

What Is The Fear Of Flying

"In time we hate that which we often fear"

Shakespeare (Antony & Cleopatra)

If you have a fear of flying, you are not alone. It has been estimated that, in Canada and the United States at least nine percent of those who can afford to travel by air are unable to do so due to a fear of flying. This represents ten to twelve million potential air travel customers and immeasurable anxiety and stress.

The fear of flying goes under a variety of names: Aviaphobia, Flight Phobia, Airplane Phobia, Fearful Flying or White Knuckle flying. Whichever term is used the meaning is the same; an all-pervasive fear associated with flying in an aircraft. The consequences of this fear can range from mild discomfort all the way up to blind panic, and can often lead to a complete avoidance of air travel. In this book I will refer to the fear as flight phobia and to the sufferer as the fearful flyer.

The fearful flyer will often feel frustrated and angry, because of what he or she sees as a foolish fear. Yet, the fear itself is painful and very real and may often be greater than the desire to fly. In this case, the fearful flyer will avoid flying at all costs and will seek alternative forms of transportation rather than face the very painful experience of travelling by air. The problem is that, paradoxically, each time they take the easy choice of avoiding flying, their lives become more complicated.

Some people will go to extreme lengths to avoid flying. In doing so, they become locked in a spiral of greater and ever more involved rationalizations, explanations and justifications for their behaviour. The anxiety surrounding their flight phobia is thus increased rather than decreased. Take the case of Eda, for example. Eda had been running a successful business for several years. The business necessitated her having to make frequent business trips to various places in Canada and the United States. All was well until, at the very height of her success, Eda developed a fear of flying. It was a fear so great that eventually she refused to set foot on a plane. Not one to give up, Eda took to the highways and began driving to all her business meetings. She soon found that she was spending more time on the road than she was on her business. To ease the load, her husband was enlisted to help with the driving, but that took him away from his business and created a whole new set of problems. By the time I saw her, she was so exhausted from the strain of all that driving, added to the pressures of running her business, that she had serious doubts as to whether she could continue. She was on the verge of giving it all up. Once she had confronted her phobia, and worked hard to overcome it, she was once again truly in control. She began working smarter rather than harder.

Or take the case of Ted. Ted was a retired aircraft mechanic who had worked on planes all his life. He had flown many hours but always in propellor driven planes. Because he was unfamiliar with jets, he claimed not to trust them. Upon retirement, Ted spent half of his year at his winter home in Southern California. This entailed a drive of several thousand miles, much of it over icy roads and through unpredictable and often treacherous mountain passes. He had been doing this for several years, but was getting older and didn't know how much longer he would be able to make the difficult drive every year. The obvious answer was to fly, but he simply would not step on a jet plane. Again, once Ted had confronted his phobia, he became an ardent and enthusiastic flyer who will be able to winter in California for many more years.

In avoiding flying, fearful flyers find that they have to explain the reason for their avoidance to other people or make excuses to justify their different behaviour. They risk being laughed at, being considered weak or, at the very least, having to undergo some teasing and shaming. Their self-esteem suffers and they become angry with themselves. Other people can never be trusted to be understanding of their problem. On the other hand, if they are fortunate enough to have an understanding and supportive partner or set of friends, this can make all the difference in their attitude toward flying.

Nobody is exempt from flight phobia. It affects men and women equally regardless of profession or life-style. It can strike sports figures, entertainers, politicians, business people, travel agents, even airline crew members. It can affect people who travel for their living, people who travel for fun, or people who travel to enable others to travel. Anybody can develop a fear of flying.

In this modern world, no one need suffer as the result of a phobia of any kind, be it a fear of flying, dentists, or speaking in public. For every question there is an answer, and for every problem there is a solution. You *can* overcome your flight phobia if you want to. The key phrase here is "if you want to." Some people are so afraid that they are not interested in learning to eradicate their fears. If you are one of those people and you have chosen to accept your inability to fly, then it is your right as a human being to do so. We should respect your decision. However, if you say that you have accepted your inability to fly, but continue to pine, curse, wail, inflict guilt on yourself or others when you see and hear that your family and friends are flying to exotic places, or doing things without you, then your acceptance is only lip-service. It is a signal that you really do want to be free of your fears. Be honest with yourself.

In fact, the one positive thing about flight phobia is that you *can* get over it. I can't promise that you will end up loving flying, or that it will ever be listed in the top ten things you enjoy doing. However, I can be reasonably sure that if you approach the problem and the solution enthusiastically, you will learn to overcome your fear. While you may not be completely cured as a result of reading this book, it will provide you with help and point you toward the goal of flying with confidence and a new and healthier attitude.

CHAPTER TWO

What Is Flight Phobia?

"The fear of danger is ten times more terrifying than the danger itself."

Daniel Defoe (Robinson Crusoe)

Since the terms are often used interchangeably, let us examine the difference between a fear and a phobia.

Every one of us has experienced fear at some time in our lives. Fear means an uneasy feeling. It also signifies an unpleasant emotion caused by the nearness of danger or the expectation or anticipation of pain. Another definition of fear is anxiety for safety or a painful emotion caused by impending danger or evil; a state of alarm. Fear is a built-in emotional response to perceived danger. It is essential in preventing us from going blindly into threatening situations and in preparing us to respond. During the preparation of this book I was discussing the fear of flying with an associate. "I have only ever been afraid once in a plane," he said. "That was in a small float plane, piloted by a madman, over a northern lake." He went on to describe the pilot's habit of cutting across the end of a peninsula in order to save time when landing back at base. A road hairpinned around the point that was used by heavy trucks servicing a local mine. On the last day of work, the pilot made his usual approach low over the mine road. Unfortunately, this time there was a truck coming around the bend. The pilot made an emergency maneouver, narrowly missing the surprised truck driver and making everyone feel that their stomachs had been left on the road. No one was hurt, but it was some time before my friend's hands stopped shaking. He had been justifiably afraid and his body had reacted to a direct and immediate threat.

A phobia, on the other hand, is an irrational fear. A definition of the word phobia is: a lasting abnormal fear or a great dislike of something. It also means a morbid fear or aversion, apprehension or dread. The stimulus for a phobia may or may not be clear, even to the phobic. Even when the stimulus is clear, the danger that is perceived may still bear little relation to the reaction. The fearful flyers who refuse to board a plane at all, or do so in a state of high anxiety, are not reacting to any real danger. They are over-reacting out of all proportion to any real threat. Indeed, there is probably no threat to them at all. It is this disproportionate over-reaction that characterizes a phobia. A phobia will often be accompanied by morbid, irrational, immature and obsessive thoughts. It can also give rise to catastrophic thinking, such as "what if the plane crashes?" or, "what if an engine falls off?" Often a phobia is so terrifying that the sufferer will completely avoid the feared situation or thing. Phobics tend to be creative thinkers. Often, it is their overactive imaginations that gets them into trouble in the first place! Thus they are very good at coming up with creative, apparently valid reasons why they cannot fly.

WHAT IS YOUR BASE PROBLEM?

Is it just good old stress, or does it go deeper than that? Flight phobia, like any other phobia, can fall into one or all of the three main categories of phobias:

Monophobias
Cluster phobias
Social phobias

Monophobia (or single phobia).

A monophobic is someone who is afraid only of *one* thing. The phobia can be simply a learned behaviour. A flight phobia, for example, may have developed after witnessing another nervous person on a flight or in the passenger lounge prior to boarding. The phobic may have travelled with a nervous person before, or they may have experienced a previous bad flight with heavy turbulence or mechanical problems. Any of these experiences would remain in their mind the next time they flew. They may find themselves worrying that the same thing will happen again and, consequently a phobia is born.

People with monophobias are relatively easy to treat. All they usually require is a restoration of their confidence, and a reduction in their stress level.

If, for example, a flight phobic is concerned with mechanical failure or malfunctions of the aircraft, then accurate information about aircraft and flying in general, will usually dispel their fears. This was Linda's case. Linda came to see me because she was concerned about the landing gear. She worried herself into a state of near panic each time she had to fly. She was terrified that the hydraulic system in the plane would fail, the wheels wouldn't come down correctly and the plane would have to make a crash landing. After listening to a talk by an aircraft mechanic on one of our airport familiarization tours, her fears were quelled with the knowledge that there are backup systems for the landing gear. If one fails, then another will take its place. Even if all fail, the landing gear can be brought down manually by the crew. Linda was so relieved and reassured that it was never a problem for her again. She could then fly with confidence. It was the lack of information, or misinformation, that did the harm.

However, monophobia is quite rare. Most fearful flyers are more complicated than Linda. Their anxieties fall more into the areas of cluster and social phobias.

Cluster phobias

Cluster phobias, as the name implies, are more complex. They usually have more than one cause and manifest themselves in interwoven ways, forming a cluster around an apparently single stimulus. Flight phobics more frequently find their fears falling into one or more of the following cluster phobias.

Agoraphobia

Agoraphobia is commonly defined as a fear of open spaces. It is actually far more complicated. Agoraphobia is the most crippling of all the phobias. Sufferers feel as if they are afraid of everything. They cannot cope on a daily basis or lead a normal life because of ongoing fears and panic attacks. For the sufferer, travelling away from home is never easy or enjoyable and may be impossible. These people would naturally dread, and probably avoid, air travel if at all possible.

Claustrophobia

Claustrophobia, the fear of confinement or of being trapped, is also a cluster phobia. Claustrophobia, when severe, can be both crippling and limiting to the sufferer. Sufferers have particular difficulty with flying because of the confined space in the plane. In addition, they have a need for constant fresh air which represents space and freedom. Claustrophobia derives from feelings of being entrapped, physically and/or emotionally. The need for complete or utter control is at the core of claustrophobia.

Acrophobia

Acrophobia, the fear of heights, is also a cluster phobia. The victim often feels terrified that they may slip, fall, or be pushed when in a high place such as a ledge, a step-ladder, a roof, or a balcony. They also feel uncomfortable in high-rise buildings, particularly disliking floor-to-ceiling windows. They often experience a drawing sensation and feel disoriented when they attempt to look out or down from a high place. The sufferer may not only avoid flying, but also buildings which they consider too tall. They will feel panicky being close to a window overlooking anything with a drop outside. There is, usually, an element of claustrophobia as well. The sufferer feels trapped by the height, especially if escape from the situation (for example, the use of an outside fire escape) would expose them to even greater fear.

Acrophobics often dislike bridges, especially those with open slats or spaces in the floor. They will usually avoid such things as gondolas, chair lifts, windowed elevators, mono-rails and carnival rides such as ferris wheels or roller-coasters. They are safety conscious people.

While some flight phobics fear height itself, others simply fear falling or drowning. Many dislike the thought of being suspended in the air, with nothing solid underneath them.

Cluster phobias are all encompassing. They are related to deeper emotional and psychological problems, such as the fear of separation from one's security and the absence of familiar people, places or things. All of these are, in turn, related to one's self esteem and feelings of being out of control, loneliness, abandonment, death, illness or personal injury. The whole process of flying is more difficult for cluster phobics because of the generalized feelings of anxiety which are experienced in many everyday situations. For these people, anxiety and discomfort can be experienced in such things as congestion in the air terminal, customs halls, security checks and procedures, waiting areas, elevators, escalators and moving sidewalks. Some tend to worry about peripheral areas of the flight, such as the layout of the terminal at their destination; wanting to know how to get out as quickly as possible, the location of the car rental booth, taxi stands or the airport bus. Even the layout of their hotel can be important to them. Which floor will they be staying on? Are they close to an exit?

Social phobias

Individuals with severe social anxieties such as shyness, poor interpersonal or conversational skills, or those who simply feel uncomfortable at close proximity to other people, often have difficulty on airplanes. The other passengers make them nervous.

Social phobics suffer from low self-esteem. They have learned to feel badly about themselves and often have high levels of guilt and/or shame. They worry about being appropriate and being judged. They are concerned with the opinions of others. Social phobics fear the scrutiny of others. For them, the worst thing that can happen is to have other people witness their nervousness and judge them as inferior. In a flight situation, the social phobic can feel trapped and unable to get away from what they fear the most, people.

TYPES OF FLIGHT FEARS

As we have seen, the fear of flying is not just a simple fear of going up in an aircraft. Flight phobia actually encompasses four categories of fear. A flight phobic may experience just one of them, a combination of them, or all of them, and not necessarily at the same time:

The fear of impending disaster

This fear is, perhaps, the easiest for both the phobic and the non-phobic to understand, for it does reflect a real danger, however slight that may be. Simply put, this is the fear of the plane crashing. Few travellers do not suffer some degree of anxiety in the knowledge that planes do sometimes crash, and that, looked at rationally, the chances of survival in a plane crash are not always good.

Observing passengers on a plane, particularly during the first stages of take-off, you may notice how even the most seasoned or apparently calmest of them will show some signs of tension. A businessman will open his briefcase and become

engrossed in his papers. People will bring out books and magazines to take their mind off of the take-off. However, once the
plane is safely off the ground they seem to lose interest in their
activities. Others may exude an outward appearance of calm,
leaning back in their seats, making themselves comfortable.
But look closely, their arms may be crossed tightly, or their
hands may grip the seatrest. Everyone is aware at this critical
time. It is quite normal to be a little tense during take-off. Paradoxically, many flight phobics tend to accept the real danger
and instead focus their fears on less easily defined stimuli, such
as:-
• sudden or unexpected sounds or changes in sound patterns
   that may indicate a malfunction with the plane,
• fear that, if the engines stop, the plane will plummet to the
   earth like a lump of lead,
• fear that the pilot will suffer a heart attack or food poisoning
   and will be unable to control the plane,
• fear that lightning will strike the plane and cause a fire,
• fear of an unexpected announcement, particularly in regard
   to a malfunction,
• fear that an engine will fall off, or that a tire will blow.

The Fear of Being out of Control or Powerless

   A person tends to be less afraid of a situation over which
he or she has control or power. The fear of being out of control
says to the phobic that, should something go wrong, they can
not control what would happen. They do not have the upper
hand. It is like sitting in the passenger seat of a car when somebody else is driving. Most drivers much prefer to be in control
of the car and feel more tense or nervous as a passenger. A
flight phobic would be much happier flying the plane himself,
or even sitting on the pilot's knee! Feeling out of control elicits
stress and anxiety. Many fearful flyers consider obtaining a
pilot's license as a way of combating their fears.
   In the fear of being out of control, fears focus on such
things as:
• lack of trust in the pilot's judgment or in his ability to fly the
   plane safely,
• not being able to see where the plane is going,
• changes in sound, such as the sound of the flaps being
   activated or the landing gear coming up or down,
• the sight of movement in the wings or sudden movements of

the plane, as may be experienced during turbulence,
- the sight of the pilot or any member of the flight crew walking through the passenger compartment. (The terrified and, by now, suspicious phobic thinks, "Why is *he* walking through here, why doesn't he go back and fly this thing?),"
- anybody walking about during the flight, especially large and heavy people, children playing in the aisles, line-ups for the washrooms, all of which could, in their mind, cause the plane to be out of balance. (The phobic might think, in these situations, "why don't they all just sit down and keep still? The plane will tip over!") Many fearful flyers will not move from their seats for any reason during a flight, not even to visit the washroom.

The Fear of Being Confined (Claustrophobia)

As described earlier, Claustrophobia is the fear of being shut in, of being unable to escape from the situation. Claustrophobic fears focus on such things as:
- knowing the door is closed and that it is physically impossible to re-open it once the plane is airborne,
- being restrained by the seat-belt,
- sitting in close quarters,
- entering the washrooms,
- too many people surrounding them,
- lack of fresh air,
- feeling exposed and vulnerable because there is nowhere to hide or to run for safety,
- people walking in the aisle blocking their "escape route."

The Fear of Heights, Falling or Drowning (Acrophobia)

Acrophobia is the fear of high places. Acrophobics will avoid window seats, or will immediately draw the shade, as they are reluctant to look out of the window. They do not want to know how high they are, or what is, or is not, underneath them. They fear that, if indeed the plane should fall from the sky, they would remain conscious throughout, and dread the thought of the helpless feeling that would accompany the fall to the ground or the water below. Acrophobics usually dislike the sensation of the plane banking.

As a person who is afraid to fly, you may identify with just one of these four categories, or you may find yourself identifying with elements of all of them. But the fear of flying is nonselective. If you feel that your fear stems from just one of these categories, the fear of boarding that aircraft is just as intense as if it stemmed from all four. You are a fearful flyer. In the following chapter I will discuss how fearful flyers, like their fears, fall into several categories.

PHYSICAL SYMPTOMS OF THE PHOBIC

Faced with the feared situation, the fearful flyer will experience a high level of anxiety which, in turn, can produce physical changes in his or her body. It is these physical changes which distress the phobic. They find them very unpleasant and will try to avoid them as much as possible.

It is not possible to get a true measurement of the intensity of feelings of anxiety, any more than it is possible to obtain the true measurement of pain. Everyone's pain tolerance level, or threshold, is unique - we cannot compare our intensity to another's but only the feelings of anxiety themselves. What is torture to you may only be mild discomfort to someone else.

Feelings of anxiety can range from mild symptoms, such as sweaty palms, all the way up to a full-blown panic attack. Table 1 below lists some of the most common physical symptoms exhibited by fearful flyers.

TABLE 1

Some of the physical symptoms which fearful flyers often complain about experiencing. All are not necessarily experienced at any one time.

- increased muscle tension
- "fidgety-ness"
- a sinking feeling in the stomach
- weakness in the limbs, "jelly legs"
- frequent urination
- dry mouth
- flushed feeling
- tension headache
- tremulousness - internal or external
- tingling and/or numbness in the arms or legs
- light-headedness
- shortness of breath
- dizziness
- faintness
- restlesness
- general uneasiness
- "knots" in the stomach
- loose bowel movements, diarrhoea
- nausea
- moist palms
- feeling drained and pale, blanching
- increased heart rate
- "butterflies" in the stomach
- constricted feelings in the chest
- detached feelings, disorientation
- irregular heartbeats
- clamminess
- pounding pulse

If you do suffer from anxiety symptoms, you should discuss them with your doctor. Many of the symptoms can also have organic origins and may not necessarily be the result of anxiety alone.

A panic attack is when most of the feelings in Table 1 may occur at once, and the sufferer undergoes several minutes of sheer terror. Because most of the symptoms are physical, they may fear they are having a heart attack or a seizure of some kind. They may become afraid because they think that they are becoming terribly ill or that they are going to die on the spot. They may feel sure that they are completely losing control or about to pass out or go crazy. During the panic attack, the sufferer usually wants to escape from the situation and these unpleasant physical feelings. A large part of their fear is that the people around them may witness the attack and its accompanying behaviour. Afterwards, they may remain terrified that the feeling will re-occur. They will be embarrassed at the scene which they feel they have created. Unfortunately, some people who bolt feel so humiliated that they refuse to get back on the plane and, in some cases, never fly again. I can assure you that nobody has ever gone crazy, had a heart attack, or died, due to a panic attack. Nevertheless, a good deal of re-assurance is necessary in such a situation and a kind, understanding support person can be of great assistance. It is not uncommon for a fearful flyer to feel so panicky that as they approach the plane they are about to board that they literally freeze. It is as though their body has turned to stone or ice. All of their muscles constrict and refuse to move. They feel immobilized by fear.

Many flight phobics have been known to board the plane, only to become increasingly anxious and frightened as the door closes and the plane begins to move. It is at this point that they may beg to get off. While the captain of the plane prefers not to deviate from his original flight plan, he would much prefer to let a distressed person off the plane. He certainly doesn't want to make anyone stay on board against their will. If at all possible he will stop and arrange to have the fearful flyer deplaned.

Not every fearful flyer has a panic attack. Some may experience only mild anxiety during their travels. Yet, the feelings may be disturbing and constant enough to cause them to worry about flying and, in some cases, to avoid flying altogether. Associating flying with these uncomfortable feelings, they soon learn to approach it with trepidation.

PHOBIAS CAN BE CURED

Most flight phobics are taken by surprise when they first experience an anxiety or panic attack. Like a bolt from the blue it seems to arrive from nowhere and strike with a tremendous, terrifying force. It is the memory of this first anxiety or panic that makes it difficult to overcome the anxiety. Although some will go on flying, hoping that it will never happen again, they will keep themselves in a state of apprehension and anxiety, wondering if and when it will reoccur. That, in itself, can become a self-fulfilling prophecy.

Phobias are unpredictable, and for the sufferer they make no sense at all. They just seem to be an uncontrollable force.

Under therapy conditions, people usually admit to having experienced anxieties in other areas of their lives prior to their first big attack. However, they felt these anxieties were manageable and not overwhelming so they simply carried on with their lives, either avoiding the situations that bothered them, or rationalizing that the unpleasant feeling was only occasional and could be lived with. For example, having developed an uncomfortable, anxious feeling when riding in an elevator, the budding phobic may begin to avoid elevators. They will attempt to justify this by convincing themselves that they need to lose weight, or that they need to stay in shape. They will begin to insist on taking the stairs each time they are faced with an elevator ride. They will say this is for their health and deny that the use of the stairs is their way of avoiding the feelings of anxiety. They will laugh if anyone suggests that fear might be the cause of their increased activity.

These anxieties are not interfering with their life, as flying avoidance may. It isn't until afterwards that they can see that the phobia didn't just happen. It had been building for some time. They had simply refused to acknowledge the warning signs. There is always a reason for a phobia.

One vital ingredient *must* be present before a phobia can take hold. The individual must have been operating at a very high stress level. It is stress and an over-reaction to a situation that help to create a phobia.

CHAPTER THREE

Stress And Its Role In Fearful Flying

"Stress is essentially the rate of wear and tear in the body."

Dr. Hans Selye.

WHAT IS STRESS?

Stress is a part of life, without a reasonable level of stress we cannot be productive. Stress can provide us with motivation, as well as a feeling of vibrancy and aliveness. Stress can also be seen as our built-in alarm system, or as a safety valve. If we understand stress and use it to our advantage, it can help us to live full, exciting and healthy lives. Unfortunately, many people go through life not fully realizing that they have very high levels of stress. These people wonder constantly why they are so strung out, fearful, anxious, vulnerable to illnesses and feeling blue or depressed.

There are two types of stress. Let's examine them by way of some examples.

Positive stress

Most people view stress as a negative concept. Yet, it can be a very positive factor in our lives. It is the effect of stress on your body and mind that enables you to react swiftly when faced with a crisis. The sudden onrush of stress causes you to react quickly when a child darts into the road in front of your car, allowing you to react rationally when that is exactly what is required. In that crisis situation, your mind takes over at once, invoking the physical actions required to force on the brakes and bring your car to a stop. Your stress works for you in that situation.

Let us imagine that you are expecting guests to arrive for dinner in a few minutes. You are running late and there are still several details to attend to. Again, it is stress in the situation that gives you that extra boost, that extra ounce of energy that allows you to quicken your pace and meet your deadline without being overly frazzled.

Positive stress is relatively harmless and is frequently pleasurable, providing a feeling of being energized and alive.

Negative stress

Stress becomes negative only when we deny it or when we try to pretend that it does not exist and allow it to build to unmanageable proportions in our minds and bodies. In this circumstance, the body and mind frequently have to find their own way of taking a break from the stress they are enduring. They do this by creating a crisis of their own, such as high anxiety and a panic attack.

How do we know when we are feeling stressed?

Our bodies react when we are in situations which our minds perceive as threatening. All kinds of physical changes occur simultaneously as our built-in safety alarm rings. Our sensory organs, principally our sight and hearing, receive the signal of alarm and pass it on to the brain. From there, messages are sent through the nervous system to the muscles and other organs. The muscles contract, often very suddenly. If the state of arousal continues, muscle tension will remain high in order to prepare you to react quickly to any further stimuli. The heart rate tends to change. In some people, blood pressure can rise to very high levels, while in others it can fall equally drastically.

Blood vessels in muscles open up, allowing more blood to flow through, while those in the abdomen and the skin contract, decreasing the blood flow. The effect is to divert blood from the skin and intestines to the muscles in the torso and limbs in preparation for greater muscular effort.

Sweating increases in fairly specific areas such as around the mouth and nose, the temples, the armpits, between the legs and, especially, the palms of the hands and the soles of the feet.

Saliva dries up. Secretion of gastric acid increases and the gastro-intestinal tract is noticeably affected, although the normal movement of the actual stomach may reduce. The intestines become more active and may gurgle, churn or rumble. There may be an urge to open one's bowels and, in a severe fright, loss of control may occur. The bladder is affected similarly. There is an urge to pass water as the bladder muscle increases its activity.

Hormonal changes occur also, but at a slower rate. Adrenaline and noradrenaline, the most important hormones involved in the stress response, become incorporated into the bloodstream and act on many of our organs. It is these hormones entering our systems that control the physical changes outlined above. In addition, adrenaline affects the metabolic balance of the body. It prepares energy reserves in the liver and muscles, making glucose available for immediate energy demands.

These physical changes, occurring in rapid succession prepare our bodies for a sudden increase in activity. This is the so-called "fight or flight response." Sometimes this phenomenon is referred to as the "adrenaline rush." We could equally well call it a stress attack, or an anxiety attack in the case of a very anxious person.

If our bodies are kept in a constant state of negative stress our health, physical, mental and emotional, will suffer as a result. The body and mind can take only so much wear and tear before they begin to break down. It is no different from an automobile that is not maintained properly. Without proper fuel and service on a regular basis, it will let you down, and costly repairs will be the result. The same principle applies to our bodies and minds.

Stress Signals

Everyone has their own signals of stress. It pays to recognize them so something can be done in time. Once the stressor, the cause of our stress, is removed then the stress itself should dissipate. While we discussed the adrenaline rush earlier, here are some other common stress signals.

Change in eating habits

Everyone is different. Some fearful flyers may stop eating when they are worried or stressed about an upcoming flight. They become so uptight that they are either disinterested in food altogether, or feel that the food just wouldn't go down or stay down. Others may want to dive into food when they feel upset and will eat anything that isn't pinned down. Some may become selective, heading for the doughnuts, chocolate bars or chips. Some people like crunchy foods, while others choose softer foods to comfort them.

Change in drinking habits

Coffee drinkers may notice that their intake increases when they are stressed about flying. Coffee, regular tea, chocolate and colas all contain caffeine. Many people do not realize that they are addicted to caffeine, and use it as a stimulant. Too much caffeine in our bodies can cause a jangly, edgy feeling, making us jumpy and nervous, only serving to accentuate the other symptoms of stress. If we become too stimulated, our sleeping patterns can be effected. Too much caffeine can keep us awake or cause stomach upsets. Nutritionists recommend that we keep our daily caffeine intake to a minimum in order to avoid these side effects. It is probably not a good idea to have coffee after about 3 p.m. Alcohol users may notice an increase in their consumption when preparing for a flight. The airport lounges are full of people trying to relieve their stress by drinking. Many alcohol users fail to recognize that alcohol is a depressant. While the immediate effects of alcohol in the bloodstream are to give the user a high, the after-effects will cause the mood of the user to plummet. All things in moderation. A drink or two can relax us, but if we go overboard we will pay the price in the form of remorse, embarrassment or a hangover. We may feel that it deadens the pain temporarily but, in reality, it simply delays it. The stress or problems remain long after the effects of the alcohol have worn off.

Need for more tranquillizers

People who use muscle-relaxants or tranquillizers may find that the prescribed daily dose just isn't doing the trick and feel the need to increase their dosage. They just can't relax prior to or during a flight.

Increase in smoking

When smokers are experiencing stress they often find that their smoking increases as well. They may light a cigarette, take a few puffs and then stub it out, only to light another. It is something physical to do to relieve the tension. Stress can produce chain smoking. That is why so many fearful flyers are upset about smoking regulations in airports and on the aircraft.

Change in sleep patterns

Stress often produces poor sleeping patterns, such as restlessness, wild and vivid dreams, or heavy, deep sleep. It may cause us to wake in the early hours, unable to go back to sleep due to an overactive mind, worry, or anticipatory anxiety. It may also cause insomnia, the inability to go to sleep. Many fearful flyers complain of sleep disturbances prior to their flight.

Headaches

While we cannot blame all headaches on stress, tension can bring on headaches. Tension headaches are usually accompanied by a dull pain and a tight sensation like a band around the scalp or neck. They affect the whole head not just one side. They are sometimes referred to as muscle contraction headaches.

Migraine headaches are in a different category. Migraines can be triggered by many different things, such as a change in altitude or weather, or certain foods, as well as stress or exhaustion.

Change in libido

People often experience a lack of interest in sex, or a drop in their libido, as a result of their stress. Once the stress is reduced, their normal frequency returns. Many people do not know that sex is a natural tranquillizer.

Other tell-tale stress signals:

- skin eruptions
- nail-biting
- constantly touching or scratching the face
- fidgeting with money, keys or jewellery
- coughing unnecessarily
- repeated blinking
- hunching the shoulders
- drumming the fingers
- tapping or jiggling the feet

• frequently biting or licking the lips
• repeated swallowing
• pulling or tugging at one's hair
• incessant talking
• shakiness or tremors
• twitching, tics
Note: You should make sure to check with your doctor to confirm that you are experiencing stress symptoms, and not some latent physical problem.

HOW DO WE GET STRESSED?

There are two reasons why people become stressed:
One: Stress usually starts when many life events occur at once or over a relatively short period of time.

Example: You are getting married, buying a new home, relocating and starting a new job - all within the next few weeks. While individually these events promise to be exciting and happy, in combination they could easily produce high levels of stress for you and for your partner. Handling just one of these events would create a certain level of stress, but probably at a manageable level. The combination of all four happening at the same time, could easily be overwhelming. Each life event presents its own problems and challenges and everyone deals with them in their own way.

Example: Your sales position is not going well. Sales are down and your job is threatened because of it. On top of that, things are not good at home, you and your spouse are not hitting it off and you have some financial difficulties that just won't go away. Then, just this morning, the boss informed you that you are expected to fly to Halifax next Monday and that while you are there he expects you to pull up those sales figures, or let him know the reason why!
At this point you begin to feel as though you can't take any more. Your anger rises and the next thing you know you're blowing up at your secretary for some minor error. On the way home some fool of a driver cuts you off and you erupt into a blind rage. You shout at the kids when they get in your way at home. You feel depressed, reach for a drink, a cigarette or food as a way of numbing the pain. It has all became too much for you. You feel pressured, overwhelmed and out of control. A likely candidate for developing a fear of flying. The flight to

Halifax may very well be that last straw.

Two: The second reason why people become stressed is because they are spoon-fed stress at an early age.

Anyone who has been raised in a chaotic household may be so used to feeling the symptoms of stress that it will take stress attacks (anxiety attacks or panic attacks), to bring it to their attention. For these people, stress is a way of life. Stress prevails for anyone raised in a violent household or in an alcoholic or a mentally abusive environment. People who have to deal with terminally ill or handicapped family members also live with stress, as do those who live with criticism, perfectionism, or over-protectiveness. Stress levels in our homes are the foundation on which we base our stress management skills. We tend to role-model our reactions to events. That is how we learn to cope with life. It follows that if a parent was highly strung, neurotic and an over-reactor, we too would probably learn to deal with life in the same irrational way. If, on the other hand, the parent was relaxed, laid back and "cool," we could well adopt this unruffled approach to life ourselves. Be realistic about your stress roots!

We are all individuals and we all view stressful situations differently. What may be stressful to you, may not necessarily be stressful to me. No two people are the same. Stress is simply the level of tension, anxiety, or general discomfort in the body as a result of feeling pressured, overwhelmed, or out of control.

HOW TO READ YOUR STRESS WARNING SIGNALS

Whenever we feel emotionally disturbed, tired, exhausted, pressured or unwell, we also feel vulnerable. If we have a fear of flying and a history of stress, then it is at these times that stress and anxiety may reappear as warning signals. If we read the signals and act upon them, our stress will subside. Our stress level is like a personal warning signal, an indicator of the pressures building up inside.

It is important, in being a successful flyer, to know when your warning signals are flashing. As your personal alarm is activated your ability to relax will become increasingly more difficult due to the boost in your adrenalin production.

When feelings have been denied for a long time, it takes a conscious effort, and a lot of practice, to clue in to them. Becoming proficient at spotting stressors, and learning to read your stress warning signals, will help you to fly in comfort and with the greatest of ease.

Lisa learned the hard way. She came to see me because of her fear of flying. She had managed to overcome much of her fear and she and her husband had planned a two week vacation without their two teenage children. Her outbound flight was uneventful and comfortable for her. She felt calm, relaxed and excited. She was pleasantly surprised and was even able to enjoy being away without worrying about the return flight home or the children. Toward the end of their holiday they talked to the children on the telephone, only to learn that their sixteen year old daughter had taken the family car out for a drive, without permission, and had been involved in an accident. Fortunately she was not harmed, but neither Lisa or her husband were too impressed and couldn't wait to get home to sort everything out. Lisa began to feel angry and guilty for being away. She also felt out of control and very worried. Her warning signals were flashing. She ignored them and paid the price.

Because of her newly acquired stress and anger, the return flight was not pleasant and Lisa felt very disappointed in her performance. Once we had the opportunity to discuss it she saw clearly how she over-reacted and became stressed. If only she had paid attention to the warning signals and changed her thinking, her flight home would have been much more comfortable. She was naturally concerned about her family but, by accepting the facts that her daughter was unharmed, the car was insured, and that they would handle the situation once they arrived home, she could have had a much more relaxed and enjoyable return flight.

Lisa did not lose any of her confidence over this incident because she soon realized that she had brought anxiety upon herself by over-reacting and by not listening to her personal alarm. She intends to fly again, but no doubt next time she will take the car keys with her!

In a similar case, Dale had to fly quite regularly on business. He was working hard to conquer his fear of flying and was beginning to experience less stress, and find more confidence, each time he flew.

Dale managed very well on a trip to his company's head office. He felt relaxed and comfortable and arrived fresh and free from stress. It was during his time in head office that Dale heard, through the company grapevine, that a job he was being groomed for was going to be given to someone else. This came as a shock to him and immediately he began to feel angry, hurt and rejected. He even began to catastrophize about his future with the company.

Dale over-reacted and became carried away with his catastrophic thoughts. His alarm was activated and he ignored it. On the return trip, the plane went through some heavy turbulence and he began to experience some of his old anxiety returning. He was disappointed but, once he had arrived home, he was able to start making sense of what had happened. He remembered what he had learned in therapy - there is always a reason for anxiety; it doesn't just happen. The news about his promotion was only rumour, nobody in authority had indicated any change in plan. In fact, his boss had commended him on his sales performance and had made no mention of any dissatisfaction. He began to realize that he had reacted to gossip and that he should be assertive and ask his boss if there was any truth to the rumour thereby putting an end to his worries. By placing a call to his boss and asking him directly where he stood with the company, Dale was soon reassured.

He was angry with himself for ruining another flight, but he did learn the valuable lesson of listening to his personal stress signal before flying. He did not lose his confidence. In fact, he looked forward to his next trip to head office as an opportunity to try again with a positive attitude. He remembered to be assertive and not to fly with any emotional clutter.

IT'S O.K. TO ADMIT THAT YOU'RE NERVOUS

As you begin to show signs of becoming less fearful about the thought of flying, change the word fearful to nervous. Somehow, nervous sounds more normal and its connotation is less negative. Most people don't fly every day and anything that we don't do on a regular basis can create tension or nervousness. If you asked twelve people sitting in the passenger lounge waiting for your flight how they honestly felt about getting on the plane, the chances are good that most, if not all, would admit to a little nervousness. Not because they are fearful flyers anticipating a disaster, but simply because they haven't boarded a plane for some time. They may be afraid of appearing stupid if they sit in the wrong seat, or they may be shy and worried about whether the person sitting next to them will be overly chatty. Others may have never flown before and find the whole procedure intimidating because everybody else seems to know what they are doing. If you are a recovering fearful flyer, it's O.K. for you to be nervous as well. In fact, you'll feel a whole lot better if you admit out loud that you are. Admitting that you are nervous is not something to be ashamed of.

Many fearful flyers are so confused about their feelings that often they don't really know what feeling they are experiencing and use words like anxious, fearful, or panic-stricken as catch-all phrases to describe their physical reactions to a stressful situation. Remember, whether we experience joy or sorrow, pain or fear, excitement or astonishment, the physical reaction to these feelings will be the same - the adrenalin rush. It will be our thinking that will determine whether we handle the situation rationally or irrationally, with panic or with excitement.

When you are beginning to work on eliminating your fear of flying, try to use the correct words that best describe how you are actually feeling. Is it really fear or simply good old nervousness? Is it nervousness or is it excitement? Maybe you're both nervous and excited! Doesn't that sound better than, "I'm phobic," or, "I'm panicky?" Admit your true feelings to yourself, and then say what you really feel. Simply doing this will help you to adopt a new and healthier attitude toward flying.

CHAPTER FOUR

How And Why Do Flight Phobias Develop?

"Fear is often an indication I am avoiding myself"

Hugh Prather

The fear of flying can surface at any age or at any stage in life. Many people have never flown at all, being too fearful to try it. They have developed a pre-conceived idea of how they think it might be and have painted themselves such a frightening picture that they simply avoid trying it altogether.

Some fearful flyers develop their phobia as the result of an unpleasant experience during a previous flight (such as severe turbulence, a heavy landing, an aborted take-off or landing, mechanical failure, poor visibility and so on). Usually, their fears are the result of being highly stressed and in an unpleasant situation. They may not understand what is happening at the time. We usually fear the unknown more than the familiar and we desperately need to feel in control of ourselves.

Some people have been normal passengers until they got married or became parents. Once they felt the responsibility and dependency of another person on them they began to fear the possibility of being unable to fulfil their new roles, especially as parents. The death of a parent in a plane crash would certainly alter the course of their child's life. Some young parents worry about another person rearing their child, and the thought is so devastating that putting themselves into what they consider a dangerous situation, such as flying in an airplane, is too much. Often these worried parents have experienced a sad, lonely or traumatic childhood themselves and cannot bear the thought of the same unhappiness for their own children.

Sometimes a fear of flying can develop by travelling with another fearful flyer. A nervous parent who makes negative comments about flying or allows their fears to show through their neurotic behaviour, will cause their children to question whether flying is such a good idea. We can learn to be afraid through role modelling.

A person already suffering from other phobias, such as claustrophobia or agoraphobia, would obviously find the physical aspect of flying very difficult for them to do in comfort. Attempting to fly with their already high anxiety and fears will, in all probability, add a new phobia to their repertoire - the fear of flying!

There are many theories on why, or how, phobias develop.

GENETIC THROWBACKS OR PHOBIC DISPOSITION ?

Some experts in the field think that phobias may derive from a genetically linked phenomenon and that phobias can run in families, passed on from one generation to the next. They speculate that certain individuals are predisposed to fears and phobias. That is why one member of a family may be liable to become fearful while other family members seem to float through life without any such difficulties.

As children, their parents have described these individuals as being overly sensitive, highly strung, timid or anxious, responding dramatically to certain sounds, sudden movement, or changes in their environment. Their central nervous systems appear to be generally more sensitive because it takes less of a stimulus to set them off. In other words, these individuals simply seem to be born this way.

Hormonal imbalance

This theory says that the cause may be related to a hormonal imbalance. Research is still underway in both of these areas, but to date nothing conclusive has yet been found to back either theory.

Inner ear malfunctions

Some clinicians believe that damage to the inner ear can cause phobias and anxieties. Certainly, if you have problems with vertigo, dizziness or motion sickness, it is always wise to have your ears checked by a specialist. It is not difficult to see that dizziness of any kind would easily produce anxiety and, if severe enough, it could develop into a phobia. There is no evidence that anxiety causes inner ear problems, unless, of course, the stress of the phobia awakens a latent ear problem.

Learned behaviour

The behaviourist school believes that all phobias are a learned behaviour. They believe that we can learn inappropriate behaviours at any stage or phase of our lives. They see anxieties and phobias as neurotic habits which, like any habits, can be unlearned.

Psychological approach

This approach focuses on the background of the phobic. It examines general insecurities - both past and present - as well as emotional patterns and an overall approach to life. These early life experiences are seen as a breeding ground for neurosis.

HOW FEARS AND PHOBIAS DEVELOP

There is always a reason for your anxiety. It *never* just happens. As I said earlier, in order to become a fearful flyer you *must* be operating at a high stress level to begin with. The flight that did you in, or that you pinpoint as the beginning or the cause of your fear is really not to blame. That flight was probably your last straw. You need to determine why your stress level was so high at that point in your life, and why it was necessary for you to deny it, or not deal with it in some other way.

Stress will not go away by itself. You may choose to believe that, by ignoring stress, it will disappear, but it won't. On the contrary, stress stockpiles until either you defuse it by meeting it head on, or else it will try to defuse itself in the form of a panic or stress attack, or some physical or psychological ailment.

It is not difficult to see how fearful flyers try to focus on the plane and try to blame it for their distress. In fact, the fear or phobia is self-induced and has probably been building for some time. The heavy turbulence, the bumpy landing, or the flight delay was only an obvious and apparently legitimate thing to accuse.

THE MAJOR CAUSE OF STRESS

Emotional distress, or negative stress, stems from the way we think about things, not from the events or things themselves. In Hamlet, Shakespeare wrote "Things are neither good nor bad but thinking makes it so." While a fearful flyer may swear that it is being in the plane that makes him feel uncomfortable, in fact it is what he *thinks* about being in the plane that makes him feel that way. We are all constantly thinking about something and it is our thoughts that shape our moods, our responses and reactions. Only we can be responsible for our own thoughts and feelings and only we can make them positive or negative.

Whether we experience joy or sorrow, pain or fear, excitement or astonishment, the physical reaction to these feelings will be the same - the adrenalin rush. The intensity of the reaction will depend on our perception of its impact and its anticipated outcome. It is our thinking that will determine whether we handle the situation positively or negatively, rationally or irrationally.

Don dislikes flying. He particularly fears mechanical problems. From the moment the plane backs away from the terminal, until it arrives at its destination, he is suspicious of every sound, every creak or groan that is, in his mind, different. He then worries about it, saying to himself, "what if the engine fails? What if we run out of fuel? I think there's a funny noise coming from the back," and so on. The more he worries, the more upset and fearful he becomes. Whenever the pilot comes on the public address system, Don is convinced that he is about to announce that the plane is in real trouble. He relaxes a little once the pilot introduces himself and gives a time check or perhaps a weather report. But then Don's suspicious mind takes over once again. "What if the pilot is just conning us with his cheery message? Maybe that is his way of getting a coded message to the flight attendants without everyone catching on!" Don checks the flight attendants to see if they are behaving normally. "Everything seems to be alright with them," he tells himself. But he isn't convinced. He still thinks that something will go wrong, and he sits and worries and waits, in anticipation of the worst. Once the plane lands without incident Don says "I was lucky again this flight but maybe the next one won't be as good." He is already anticipating his next flight. It is not difficult to see that it is Don's negative thinking that creates the problem, not the plane itself, and it is that negative thinking that is his downfall. It is the immature and irrational thinking that promotes worry and stress. Don's imagination begins to run away with him. He starts to become sick with worry.

Worry is a feeling of stress and anxiety, ranging from a mild sensation of apprehension to feeling paralysed with fear and dread. Worry derives from fearing or anticipating the unknown, things that have not happened and in all probability will never happen.

WORRY

When we worry, we catastrophize. We have recurring, obsessive thoughts regarding future events. We worry about rejection, ridicule, disapproval, or non-acceptance. We worry about being out of control or of not being in control. Sometimes this worry involves personal injury or death. We somehow believe that worrying about something can change the order of things and that we can control the outcome of situations or events that we fear or dread. Worry offers a false belief, an illusion, about control.

Normal Worry

Everyone worries from time to time. We may worry about being late for an appointment or work, or we may be worried and concerned when someone we care for is sick or hurt. We may worry about paying our bills or our taxes, or we may worry about an upcoming examination or a test.

Normal worry is necessary. By worrying we can rationally look ahead to future problems and figure out how to handle them if and when they should materialize.

As people worry, so they can become preoccupied and forgetful. Worry always produces anxiety and stress.

My parents flew out west to visit us several years ago. It was quite an event for them as they very rarely travelled by air. My father was a very nervous flyer. On the flight, the meal was served and Dad complained about the flavour of his coffee. He said it tasted awful. My step-mother, who was a take-charge person, immediately started comparing her coffee, which was poured out of the same pot, to his. She agreed that his coffee did indeed taste different to hers. She then tasted the cream that he had used, only to discover that instead of putting the coffee cream into his cup, he had inadvertently used the salad dressing. No wonder it tasted so horrible!

Dad was so worried and uptight about flying that he had become flustered and simply didn't read the labels on the look-alike containers. When we are worried we can find it difficult to concentrate and it is then easy to become confused about even the simplest things. This is when you begin to question your sanity.

How do we learn the art of worrying?

Worrying starts early in life. What was the worry climate like in your household? Were you raised by parents who worried a lot, or fussed a lot about things? We can learn to worry by role-modelling. Another way people can become worriers is by living with insecurity and uncertainty, especially if it is constant or unpredictable. What is the worry climate like in your life today?

Projected thinking

Fearful flyers experience high anxiety through their worry by projecting their minds forward into the future. They react to these thoughts as though they are real.

Projected thinking serves as a catalyst for catastrophizing and worry by producing negative images. Another name for projected thinking is anticipatory anxiety which, again, means to feel anxious about something before it actually happens. Somehow, we feel that if we can know in advance, we will be able to control the situation and thereby prevent that something, whatever it might be, from happening,

The language of projected thinking or anticipatory anxiety consists of things like, "What if my flight is delayed?, what if I bolt from the plane and make a complete fool of myself?" or "I hate turbulence. I just know it's going to be a bumpy flight." Our imaginations take over and we paint tortuous scenes for ourselves, scenes which only serve to further elevate our already high stress levels. Our negative thoughts spiral. Take, for example, the statement "I just know something will go terribly wrong." From there the thoughts might be, "I can't bear the thought of us having to make an emergency landing, or worse, to crash! No, I don't want to step onto that stupid plane tomorrow." Already this fearful flyer is talking negatively about what they imagine will happen on their flight tomorrow! What about today? Today will be lost in the preoccupation of projected thinking. By the time this fearful flyer reaches the airport they will be a nervous wreck through worry. If, in this stressed state, they do get up the nerve to board the plane tomorrow and if they should run into some light turbulence, which is probable and quite normal, they couldn't help but see it as horrific. This would definitely be an over-reaction. By over-reacting and blowing the whole scenario out of proportion the fearful flyer would probably have convinced themselves that there was something horribly wrong, and that they should never have taken this flight in the first place. Their suspicions would be confirmed. Flying *is* dangerous! What is more, they may never want to fly again. Projected thinking feeds over-reaction because everything seems so out of control. It becomes a vicious circle. (See Figure 1, page 32)

Projected thinkers are habitual or chronic worriers. While still worrying about the flight and still obsessing and catastrophizing about it, the fearful flyer also becomes sensitized to anything and everything to do with flying.

They will be more finely tuned into aircraft sounds and more observant of regular air traffic. They may even project their mind into a plane that they see in the sky and feel anxious just with the thought of being up there. They are usually attracted to newspaper and magazine articles, or movies and documentaries, both positive and negative, about aircraft. It is as though anything to do with flying pops out at them and they worry even more, becoming more stressed and anxious. Their morbid, catastrophic thoughts preoccupy their minds and they develop tunnel vision, focusing only on the upcoming flight and their concerns about it.

One good thing about projected thinking is that the anticipating is always worse than the doing. Things seldom turn out to be anywhere near as horrendous as the sufferer imagines. Thus, when the anxious traveller reaches home, he is either elated and amazed at having made the flight in one piece, or he is completely drained and exhausted. Usually, he burns up more fuel and energy with anticipatory anxiety and projected thinking than on the actual flight itself.

Not all fearful flyers use projected thinking. Some manage to push their thoughts and worries aside until they actually enter the terminal or board the plane.

We can rationalize the old cliche that "all of the worry in the world cannot change a thing," but old habits do die hard.

The Vicious Circle of Projected Thinking

It is our overactive imaginations which lead to the
pessimistic, irrational and immature thoughts which produce:
- stress and anticipatory anxiety, which, in turn produce:
- fear, which can produce:
- a self-fulfilling prophecy: anxiety while flying!

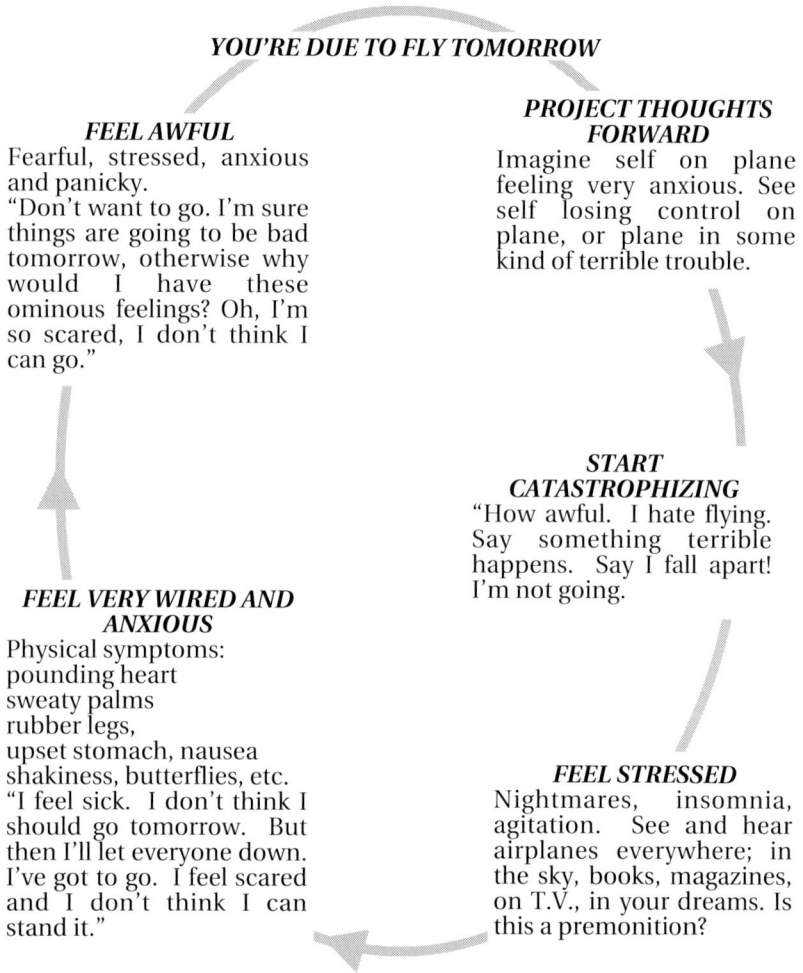

YOU'RE DUE TO FLY TOMORROW

FEEL AWFUL
Fearful, stressed, anxious
and panicky.
"Don't want to go. I'm sure
things are going to be bad
tomorrow, otherwise why
would I have these
ominous feelings? Oh, I'm
so scared, I don't think I
can go."

PROJECT THOUGHTS FORWARD
Imagine self on plane
feeling very anxious. See
self losing control on
plane, or plane in some
kind of terrible trouble.

START CATASTROPHIZING
"How awful. I hate flying.
Say something terrible
happens. Say I fall apart!
I'm not going.

FEEL VERY WIRED AND ANXIOUS
Physical symptoms:
pounding heart
sweaty palms
rubber legs,
upset stomach, nausea
shakiness, butterflies, etc.
"I feel sick. I don't think I
should go tomorrow. But
then I'll let everyone down.
I've got to go. I feel scared
and I don't think I can
stand it."

FEEL STRESSED
Nightmares, insomnia,
agitation. See and hear
airplanes everywhere; in
the sky, books, magazines,
on T.V., in your dreams. Is
this a premonition?

Figure 1

COUNTER-ATTACKING WORRY

If a large part of stress is due to worry and accompanying irrational thoughts, then the antidote would be to turn those negative thoughts into healthy, positive and mature ones. The clinical term for this process is Cognitive Restructuring. Unfortunately, it is often easier said than done. After all, it may have taken us many years to develop our negative thinking and we cannot expect to reverse the process overnight. The good news is that with practice and a conscious effort we can counter-attack worry.

What we have to understand is that we *are* in control of our thoughts and feelings and that they don't just happen. We *can* control our reactions to things.

First of all, we must decide whether the situation we are worrying about really is a calamity. If not, then we must learn to put it into it's proper perspective, and then approach it rationally and in a mature way.

If you want to fly with confidence and a new attitude then you must stop over-reacting.

THE ELASTIC BAND TRICK

Here's a quick and easy way to help counteract projected thinking and worry. Simply place an ordinary thin elastic band on your wrist. It should be comfortably loose, not so tight that it cuts off your circulation.

Whenever you find yourself projecting your mind forward with negative thoughts, simply snap the elastic band against the soft skin on the inside of your wrist. It will sting a little, and may even leave a mark. That's good. Give the band a good hard snap and at the same time tell yourself, in a firm inner voice (or out loud if you prefer), STOP! This will be a good reminder each time you do it. The slight pain from the elastic will be enough to transfer your thoughts from your worry or projected thinking to the very real stinging sensation on your wrist. In other words, the snap will break your concentration.

If you feel embarrassed about wearing the elastic band for fear that someone will notice and draw attention to it, simply tell them that you are wearing it to remind yourself of something really important. That would be the truth.

CHAPTER FIVE

What Type Of Flyer Are You?

"Only the insecure strive for security"

Anon.

J ust as there are four categories of fears involved in flight phobia, so do the phobics themselves fall into four categories, based on how they try to deal with their fears.

NON-FLYERS

This group of phobics absolutely refuse to fly under any circumstances. They will gladly spend several days driving or taking a train, bus or boat to their destination, ignoring the loss of time, the expense, and the inconvenience.

DRUG-ASSISTED FLYERS

This group will make the attempt to fly, but rely heavily on alcohol or medications like tranquillizers, Gravol or antihistamines to get them through the ordeal. Anything that they think will produce a numbing effect or make them feel drowsy becomes their flying companion.

WHITE KNUCKLE FLYERS

This group will fly without necessarily relying on alcohol or other drugs, but can suffer degrees of discomfort, stress, anxiety and dread in the process. Not usually enjoying the flying experience at all, they go through a countdown of minutes to landing. They are so tense they will literally hold on to themselves, another person, or the arms of their chair, hence the term, White Knuckle Flyers!

SITUATIONALLY FEARFUL FLYERS

This particular group of flyers may be able to relax fairly well for most of the flight. They only become upset with certain aspects of the flight procedure. For example, they may hate take-off but once that is out of the way they are fine. Others may find their fear concentrated on the landing or the period between take-off and landing. This group can pinpoint the specific areas that give them the greatest problems.

As well as the four basic coping categories, flight phobics, like all phobics, also tend to have certain other characteristics in common: obsessiveness, stress, and anxiety over return flights.

Obsessiveness

Phobic people tend to be obsessive, worry a lot and anticipate the worst. Their habits tend to be ritualistic. The flight phobic who has experienced a successful, low anxiety flight may convince themselves that it was due to the particular seat, the clothes worn, the specific airline, or the type of plane or even the way that the suitcase was packed. On the next trip they will try to get the same seat, wear the same clothes, choose the same airline and type of plane and, perhaps, pack a suitcase in the same order as the last time. If these things are not possible for the next flight, anxiety may increase. In the case of the fearful flyer, obsessiveness can almost be seen as a form of superstition.

Stress

Prior to a flight, many phobics will suffer stress symptoms, such as upset stomach or sleeplessness. They may experience nightmares, often connected to flying, with frightening or even catastrophic content. The dreams are sometimes recurring, with the same theme presenting itself over and over again, night after night. These dreams are very disturbing to the sufferer, seeming to suggest a premonitory experience.

These stress symptoms usually begin once they have made their commitment to fly, perhaps weeks before the actual flight, and will continue until their journey is complete.

Severe flight phobics often have difficulty eating or drinking while in flight, and will go for hours without food or drink. Sleep during the flight is usually not possible no matter how tired they may be. However, some phobics actually use sleep as an escape, falling asleep as soon as they are seated and waking only once the plane has touched down.

Some want only to be quiet, choosing not to talk during the flight and blocking out all conversations in order to concentrate on flying the plane. Others will talk incessantly as a means of self-distraction and a release of stress-related energy. The use of the headsets can be a means of distraction, as well as blocking out the noises and noise changes of the aircraft.

Anxiety over return flights

A nervous flyer often fears that his trip may be ruined due to a bad outgoing flight. Should they experience turbulence, or a flight delay due to mechanical problems on an outgoing flight, this frequently will unnerve them enough that they will begin to be obsessed about the return flight as soon as they have landed. They may become so fearful and apprehensive about it that, in some cases, they may even choose to abort the flight in favour of some other form of transportation. The extra cost, the loss of pride, not to mention the inconvenience, is of little concern compared to the potential pain of facing another nerve racking flight.

Others may have an uneventful outgoing flight but become obsessed about the possibility of not being so lucky twice in a row. They too, may opt for an alternate means of travel on the way home, rather than take the chance.

Usually, fearful flyers feel elated when they arrive safely at their destination. They feel as though a miracle has occurred. They may feel tempted to hug the pilot and kiss the ground.

There is no single pattern of behaviour for the phobic during a flight. People use escape mechanisms to try to overcome their feelings of anxiety and these mechanisms are as varied as the people who use them.

CHAPTER SIX

Facing Your Fear

"Nothing in life is to be feared.
It is only to be understood."

Marie Curie

F ear is an unpleasant feeling caused by the nearness of
danger or the expectation of pain.

WHAT IS YOUR BASIC FEAR?

As I said earlier, the way we think is one of the major con-
tributing factors to the fear of flying. During therapy, fearful
flyers are often surprised to learn that their actual fear is not so
much a fear of flying or of actually being in an airplane. They
come to realize that the cause of their fear has its origin in other,
deeper, and far more complex reasons. They have a basic fear.
Often, this fear can be of death, illness, separation, abandonment, rejection, social anxiety, loneliness, guilt or shame, all of
which affect one's self esteem.

For example, my client C.B. writes, "my fear of flying is
related to the confinement for a period of time in the limited
space of the airplane. Therapy made me realize that fear trans-
lates into a fear of losing control, of publicly exposing myself
should I have a panic attack or become hysterical. I think that
people will judge me as being crazy and immature. This behaviour pattern stems from a dysfunctional family background." Another client, J.E. puts it another way, "I think part
of my problem was that I had to please everyone or suffer the
consequences. That started as far back as I can remember. If
other people interfered in any way with me then I possibly
wouldn't have the results that I needed to please everyone. I
needed to be in control and when something happened that I
didn't understand or could not control, I would panic." C.E.

found the root of her fear of flying in yet another source. "I developed a fear of flying when I had to find something physical to use to hide my feelings. Getting on an airplane did that for me. I denied my desire to have fun and enjoy life believing that every aspect of life had to be under control and I was to be totally responsible." Still another example comes from L. J., who had come to me for help with her fear of flying. "My first grip of extreme fear started when I was seven years old. It was the death of an infant brother at birth. Many other griefs, bereavements and anxieties entered my life through the years and now, at the age of fifty-three, I was very fearful and had no idea how to work through these personal problems that I had always put on the back burner to talk about some other day. Then one day my problems had a label. It was unresolved grief that had controlled my life."

These examples illustrate that we need to look beyond the fear of flying itself. We have to learn to see the phobia as a smoke-screen, a convenient focus to which the fear can attach itself, obscuring the basic fear. It is always easier to have something outside ourselves on which to focus, blame, be angry at or to hate. It is easier than looking within ourselves for the real cause of our problems.

COMMON DENOMINATORS

While each fearful flyer's personal history is different and unique, common denominators usually thread throughout their stories. The two most prominent factors are, 1) that they have experienced the discounting of their feelings and, 2) that they fear, or suffer from, loneliness. These components always affect self esteem and in treatment, these two factors are nearly always present. In recovery, it really pays to know and understand your own basic fear and to become realistic about yourself. When you do this, your phobia will begin to melt away.

If you suspect that your fear of flying runs deeper than just being afraid of stepping on to that plane, then I would urge you to seek some professional counselling to help you get to the heart of the matter and to identify your real or basic fear. Releasing unwanted emotional baggage will help you discover a healthier attitude toward flying.

A COMMITMENT TO FLY

For the flight phobic, all aspects of a pending trip, not

just the actual flight, can be frightening. The very thought of any part of the flight process can invoke terror in their hearts. From the time they begin to discuss an upcoming trip, the non-assertive phobic, while externally feigning enthusiasm and going through the motions of making plans, is aware of a voice in the back of their mind saying, "No! I can't do it," or sometimes even more emphatically, "No! I don't want to do it!" But rather than appear to be a wet blanket and spoil everyone else's fun, they go along with the plans and pretend to enjoy them. Besides, somewhere beneath the lurking terror, they are aware that they really would like to take the trip. Assertive fearful flyers will just say plain "No" to a flying invitation, or "I'm really scared, but I'll give it a try."

Occasionally, a phobic will agree to go on the trip, but immediately go into a dark, sulking mood for which nobody around them can understand the reason. They are feeling entrapment. They feel trapped by their commitment and are fearful and ashamed of discussing their apprehension. From the time that they make the actual commitment to fly, through the process of purchasing the ticket, right up to the landing and exit from the airport at their destination, the entire situation is loaded with feelings of anxiety, worry, apprehension and fear.

This situation is made worse when the phobic is obliged to travel on business as a part of his or her job. Even more stress and anxiety is created by their reluctance to admit their fears or concerns to their employers. In this case it becomes a true fear - the very real fear of losing their job. In these situations, the phobic *has* to fly. For them avoidance is not possible. They feel trapped by the commitment.

It is not difficult to see why many fearful flyers turn down better jobs or promotions if the new situation exposes them to air travel. Should they confide in their families and friends the true reason for turning down the job, they run the risk of being considered a little crazy. For many fearful flyers the stakes are too high.

PART TWO

The Solution

CHAPTER SEVEN

Taking The Stress Out Of Flying

"Nothing can bring you peace but yourself."

Ralph Waldo Emerson

Having established what stress is and having some idea of how we become fearful flyers, it is now time to understand some ways in which we can take the stress out of flying and begin the journey to recovery.

In order to do this, there are four major elements that we need to address.

1. The importance of satisfactory communication.
2. The restoration of trust.
3. Letting go of the need for utter control.
4. Living in "the now."

THINGS THAT GO BUMP IN THE FLIGHT

Still another element, no less important than these four, is to understand, at least in general terms, the flight process. Obviously, this book cannot give you a complete course in aeronautics, but Section 3 addresses the most frequently asked questions about flying and provides answers from experts in the field.

THE IMPORTANCE OF SATISFACTORY COMMUNICATION

Communication is a basic life skill. Our ability to communicate will determine, in large part, our personal happiness, and may well prove to be a valuable key for the fearful flyer.

To communicate means to make known, to succeed in conveying information, to be connected or joined. Nothing is more frustrating than trying to talk with someone, only to find that they are preoccupied, opinionated, judgemental, disinterested, or so eager to talk to us, that they haven't listened to a word we have been saying. To connect with someone, even briefly, is like a breath of fresh air. We feel that someone has thought enough of us to give a little of their valuable time and energy. They have taken us seriously, boosted our self esteem and made us feel validated. When we connect or join with another human being we feel satisfied. On the other hand, if we try to connect with another and are not listened to or taken seriously, put down, criticized, ridiculed, judged, then we will walk away from the conversation dissatisfied, with our tail between our legs, feeling deprived and stressed. We all need to connect with at least one person in our lives in order to prevent severe loneliness.

Family Communications

The closer or more intimate the relationship, the greater the pain when communications collapse or break down. You would think that of all the people in the world, our families would be the safest and easiest people with whom to talk. Unfortunately, for many of us, the family unit can be one of the loneliest and most uncomfortable places in the world.

A family with poor communications can inhibit and infect each member. Inhibition produces denial of real feelings and emotions and produces a lack of spontaneity and individuality in a person.

How were the communications in your family? How are communications with your intimates today?

For fearful flyers, one of the most difficult things to do is to admit openly their fears and talk with people about how terrified they really are in the airport and on the plane. They worry that if they do, others won't understand and may laugh at them, ridicule them, or put them down because of their admissions. They will feel shame. In addition, their confessions could be thrown up in their faces at some future time or used as ammunition against them in the next argument. Therefore, it becomes much easier to deny the very existence of these feelings, pretending to others and themselves that they do not feel anything at all. So they commit to their flight, board the plane grinning and bearing it, or they make poor excuses as to why they will not fly. All the while they are wondering why they feel so misunderstood, alone, afraid, stressed and miserable. The denial of feelings feeds stress.

One of the first things we need to do in order to free ourselves from the fear of flying is to establish guidelines and boundaries to fit our own needs. We must learn to be assertive.

Loneliness

It is not difficult to see how loneliness evolves. We all need to connect with another human being in order to feel fully alive and whole. There is a pressing need for interconnection within us all.

However, forming this connection necessitates taking a risk and finding the courage to open up. In order to have trust and faith in another person we need to feel free enough to be able to ask for what we need and to share our thoughts and feelings, (which are, after all, the very essence of our being). If we do not risk and continue to live our lives safely insulated, we will never know the true feeling of intimacy and connectedness. In other words, we will feel lonely.

If we have someone that we trust and who listens to us, takes us seriously, acknowledging our feelings, then we will feel less fearful. It is wonderful to have a fan club and we all need to feel supported.

Loneliness derives from an unwillingness, or an inability, to communicate. Satisfactory communications are the antithesis of loneliness. What has loneliness to do with a fear of flying? For some, it is the root cause.

Many fearful flyers complain of loneliness, not only while flying, but also in their daily lives. Their loneliness usually stems from one of five sources:

1. A lack of anyone special in their lives with whom they can sit down and really open up.
2. The presence of someone to talk to who does not listen. They are absorbed in other things that seem more important, such as watching T.V., reading a book or the newspaper, or repairing the car.
3. Some people know how they feel inside but cannot put those feelings into words. Or, perhaps, they cannot identify their feelings at all. These lonely people usually feel frustrated and emotionally confused a good deal of the time because they cannot get out what is inside of them.
4. I have had clients say, "I have a partner who constantly wants to fix my life. I tell him how I feel and he offers me suggestions and advice but he *never* really hears what I'm saying. It's frustrating. In fact, I just give up trying to get through a

good deal of the time. What's the use?"

5. Others say that their partners are so busy talking themselves that there isn't any air-time left. They are so interested in talking that they are oblivious to others. Listening is a skill they just haven't acquired.

All of these fearful flyers will feel lonely and isolated to some degree.

Discounting

A major dysfunction in communication is the discounting of a person's feelings. All too often, especially within families, feelings are never expressed, or if they are, they are paid little attention. This can very easily produce the fear of opening up and disclosing feelings and opinions to one another.

If you are the by-product of a family or in a current relationship where feelings are discounted, you will probably have put up a wall. Perhaps you have vowed never to share your feelings with anyone ever again. You may stay that way until someone special whom you feel you can trust walks into your life.

Example 1 (Discounting)

Paul: "You won't believe this honey! The boss called me in to day and he wants me to fly to London for a convention next week."

Wife: "So!"

Paul: "So, I don't think I can handle another flight. I had such a bad time that last time. You know how scared I was."

Wife: "Paul, what kind of a man are you? I can't believe that a guy your size could be afraid of anything. Just because you were scared the last time doesn't mean it will be the same this time. Besides, you would be a fool to turn down a free trip."

You can see that Paul will soon close right down or he will become angry and defensive. He certainly would not feel satisfied.

Example 2 (Good listening)

Paul: "You won't believe this, honey! The boss called me in today and he wants me to fly to London for a convention next week."

Wife: "You don't sound too happy about that!"

Paul: "No, I'm not. I had such a bad time the last flight I took. I don't think I can handle another one."

Wife: "You're really frightened about flying this time?"

Paul: "Yes, honey, I am, and I don't know what to do about it. I feel really trapped by it all. I'm plain scared. I don't want to go, and I feel so stupid and weak."

Because Paul's wife was a good listener and listened for his feelings, she was able to reflect back what she had heard. Paul felt comfortable enough to open up even more. From this point he would be open to any suggestions or help from his wife. He would feel satisfied and loved.

During Paul's discussion with his wife he may admit that he has to go if he wants to keep his job, but at least he will be flying with his wife's love and support. That in itself is better than any tranquillizer.

Assertion

Assertiveness and good listening skills are the main ingredients for satisfactory communications. Basic assertion means to take effective action, to use one's authority or to insist on one's rights. Assertion is a definite statement that something is a fact. It means standing up for one's rights, beliefs, feelings or opinions, without degrading, humiliating or dominating another person.

Assertion is an alternative to passivity (non-assertion) or aggression (anger or hostile behaviour). To be assertive is our right as human beings. When we are being assertive we are being real. In order to be assertive we must be honest, with ourselves and with other people. To be assertive means to tell the truth.

When we are assertive we respect ourselves. It feels good to be honest and this, in turn, elevates our confidence and self esteem. We also gain respect from others by being assertive and up-front with people and by being honest with them. People know where they stand with us and they know who we are. As we express our right they will learn what we think, our beliefs and opinions and how we feel. We then have nothing to hide.

People are often afraid to be assertive for fear of offending the other person or of getting them upset or angry. They fear rejection, ridicule, conflict or confrontation and will do anything to avoid these feelings.

When we are non-assertive we pacify others in order to avoid conflict. Non-asserters tend to be overly accommodating and overly apologetic. They will defer to others' actions or opinions, appearing to have no preferences of their own. They are easily manipulated and not respected because of it. They usually have difficulty saying no.

Aggressiveness is often used as a defence mechanism (I'll get you before you get me). It is also used to cover up feelings of fear or inadequacy, throwing threatening people off the scent. Aggressive people often get their needs met by humiliating, degrading, or demeaning others. Most people do not like to tangle with someone who is explosive, so rather than confront them they will give the aggressor what they want, just to get them out of the way before too much emotional damage is done.

Assertion helps us to feel in control of ourselves, because only we as individuals know what we need, and what is important and best for us. No one should assume to know this without being told. If you want to fly with a healthy attitude speak up and assert yourself.

There are two good reasons why assertion is so important for successful flying. These can be summarized as the commitment to fly and getting our personal needs met.

THE COMMITMENT

As I have stated earlier, many fearful flyers complain of feeling discomfort and stress not only during the flight itself, but from the moment they first begin to think about flying. As soon as they feel committed to fly, they begin to experience the symptoms associated with flying itself.

When we think about flying, or having to fly, it is usually connected with one of three possible scenarios. These are recreational travel, business travel or mercy missions. Let us consider each.

Recreational travel

Recreational travel conjures up dreams of vacations, getaways, honeymoons, etc. Recreational travel may be spent with our families, lovers, friends or by ourselves. Whatever the purpose and with whomever we spend them, vacations are supposed to be stress-free and fun.

In order to make a successful vacation flight, preparation is the essential ingredient. Homework is vital. A family vacation probably originates in the living room or family room, wherever you do your family talking. Ideas for the next holiday are examined and talked about. As a person who is uncomfortable about flying, do you speak up and say what it is you would like to do, or do you meekly go along with everyone else, saying yes to plans that really don't feel right? If you don't speak up at that point, you may well be headed for trouble down the road. Non-assertion is one of the prime causes of stress and of feeling out of control. *You do not want to be stressed when you fly.* The aim is to take the stress out of flying. In this regard, being assertive right from the beginning will help a great deal.

Having been assertive with your family or friends and then having been overruled, doesn't mean that you have lost. At least you will have aired what was really in your mind. If you choose later not to go because the scenario feels too stressful for you, then that is your right also. Remember that you do not have to do anything that you don't want to do. You have choices. There is no doubt that having a phobic person in the family can, at times, be restricting to other family members. But if everyone sees it as a temporary situation that you, the fearful flyer, are working on, then most families will try to be understanding, tolerant and patient, wanting only the best for you.

The solution, or at least the best way for a fearful flyer to regain confidence, is to begin by flying under ideal, stress-free conditions. Conditions such as:
• Flying to a destination of *their* choice, with the length of flight time they feel they can handle, or feel comfortable with.
• Only going on the trip because *they really want to go*, not because they have to go.
• Having a "perfect" situation awaiting them at the other end, such as comfortable accommodation, fun, sun and relaxation.
• An ideal length of time away before the return flight home. This means not so short that any anxiety remaining after the outbound flight lingers right up to the time to return home, and not so long that anticipatory anxiety about the return flight has a chance to build to unmanageable proportions.

In other words, try to fly with as little stress as possible.

Business travel

The commitment to fly looks a little different when you are a business traveller, especially if you have not confided your fear of flying to anyone else, including your boss. The fearful business traveller finds himself in a state of constant stress. Every time his phone rings, or he receives his office mail, or he is summoned by his boss, he imagines that there will be an order for him to pack his bags and head to the airport for a company trip.

An anxious business flyer really has only two choices. One is to grin and bear it. The other is to confide in his company or boss. Most often, companies are sympathetic in such situations and the response, rather than disciplinary, is one of understanding and co-operation. Help, in the form of counselling, may even be paid for by the company. It is, after all, to the company's advantage to have calm and stress-free employees. This is not to say that all employers will react in this way, but it is worth a try.

If you are the stoic type, or a non-asserter, you will certainly have a more difficult time with business travel, because when travelling on business the company has control. Usually, travel arrangements are made for you. You may feel as though you have no choices. You simply have to go. Flying under these circumstances is really flying under duress which only adds to the stress you are already feeling.

One way to handle the situation is to tell yourself that you do have choices:

One: Tell your boss how you feel. (Should you decide not to do this, then that is another choice that you have made. Either way, the result, from a stress-reducing point of view, is the same.)

Two: Accept the fact that your fear of telling the boss is greater than your desire to fly. Now ask yourself, why are you so afraid of your boss?

Three: You have chosen the lesser of two evils. Accept that fact. Take the flight rather than fight.

Four: Flying is a part of your job. No one is making you stay in that job. Therefore, it is your choice to be there. It is neither fair nor realistic to blame anyone else for your predicament.

Mercy Missions

It is difficult enough to receive a call informing you that a family member or a friend is in trouble, seriously ill, or has passed away. Even if we expect the news, it still comes as a shock. If we intend to rush to the scene, however, it means having to make some fast decisions. For the fearful flyer, it puts them in double jeopardy. Not only do they have to deal with the situation itself, but they also have to decide on making a commitment to fly.

A recovering fearful flyer wants ideal circumstances. In the mercy situation, circumstances are usually far from ideal. Sorrow and worry might act as detractors, helping to take the focus off of yourself, but more likely they will only contribute to even more stress.

Before making a commitment to fly under these circumstances, a fearful flyer must ask themselves the following:
• do I genuinely want to be with this person in their hour of need?, or
• am I going because it is expected of me? Do I feel as though it is my duty to go? Will I feel terribly guilty if I don't go?

If you choose to go because you genuinely care, then your flight may be a lot easier than if you go out of a sense of duty or because of a feeling of guilt. Sometimes we have to put our own fears aside in order to help someone less fortunate. On the other hand, if the trip sounds overwhelming and your fear is greater than your desire to go, then it is time to be assertive. Time to say no without feeling guilty. If you are going to be riddled with guilt then, perhaps, the flight will seem the less painful of two options. The final decision and choice must be yours and yours alone, and you must feel comfortable with your decision. Remember, we always have choices. The secret is to go with what feels right for you and then to be assertive enough to verbalize your choice.

Getting our needs met

Assertiveness is a very positive tool, one that helps us to get our needs met. We need to exercise our right when we are flying in order to make the experience as comfortable as possible. We do not have to suffer, especially in silence.

A friend told me about his elderly mother who had never flown before and always professed to be afraid to try. When her daughter and grandchildren moved to Australia, flying became the only way to travel, so she decided to risk it. Her husband booked her a window seat but when they had boarded they were not put near a window. My friend's mother would not have said anything but her husband was more assertive. He complained. The flight was full, so the couple were moved into the first class area and for the entire long flight were given the royal treatment at no extra cost. My friend received a postcard from his parents saying that flying wasn't so bad after all!

Assertion means to use one's own authority. It is an expression of standing up for one's rights. You must exercise assertion, not only when making your commitment to fly, but also through all phases of the flight and journey. This is especially true when facing trouble spots or the more vulnerable aspects of the flight process.

When learning to overcome your fear of flying it is important to keep all of your plans as simple as possible. You may even have to be selfish for a few trips while your confidence builds. It is important that your support person or travelling companion is aware of your needs and is flexible enough to accommodate you.

If you prefer night travel, try to arrange a night flight. If you are claustrophobic, choose a seat on the aisle and try to avoid middle and third seats in three deep seating areas. If you dislike turbulence, choose a seat over or near the wing because there will be less bouncing there. And if the surge of power at takeoff bothers you, it may be less noticeable toward the rear of the plane.

When you need an aisle or a window seat, or prefer to sit near an exit, a washroom, over the wing, in a bulkhead seat, or at the rear of the plane - speak up. You can request your favourite seat through your travel agent when purchasing your ticket or you can arrive at the airport early enough that you can get the seat of your choice.

It is a good idea to telephone the departures information line prior to leaving for the airport to make sure that your flight is on time or that there has been no schedule change. If there is a delay you may prefer to wait in the comfort of your home rather than in the terminal. Others just prefer to get going. Dealing with flight changes can be especially hard if you have psyched yourself up only to find that plans have changed at the last moment.

If you arrive at the airport early and are left with time on your hands you can go to the departure area right away, and wait quietly there. If you prefer, you can stay in the main terminal area. You can walk around the terminal, visit the stores, have a decaffeinated drink, sit and people-watch, or go outside the terminal for a walk in the fresh air. In any case, be sure to keep an eye on the time, and know your correct departure time. For most domestic flights you need only go to the departure area twenty minutes or so prior to your flight. Your boarding time is always shown on your boarding pass.

If you prefer to pre-board, make a request at the baggage check-in or simply go forward when you hear the pre-boarding announcement.

If you would like some water to sip while on the plane, ask a flight attendant. They are there to assist you.

If you do not want a meal, it is quite alright to decline the tray when it comes. If you accept a meal and do not want to finish, it is perfectly alright to leave it. No need to feel guilty.

It can be very beneficial to let the flight attendants know that you are a fearful flyer.

Reduce your stress by asking for what you need. It will make a big difference to your attitude toward flying.

We have seen the value and importance of satisfactory communications when trying to remove stress from flying. Both assertion and good listening skills are required to make communications satisfactory and effective. To have the confidence to ask for what you need, to exercise your right as a human being, to be listened to and to be taken seriously and to have your feelings acknowledged, all help to promote stress-free flying.

CHAPTER EIGHT

The Restoration Of Confidence

"As soon as you trust yourself you will know how to live."

Goethe

T o trust means to have faith and confidence in some thing or someone. When a person develops a fear of flying, for whatever reason, one of life's basic human needs has been impaired. That need is trust.

Trust, like respect and love, is earned. Once trust is broken it takes time and history to restore it to a new and deeper level.

Trust, itself, has three components: predictability, dependability and faith. All three are necessary in order for something or someone to be deemed trustworthy. We must feel the presence of all three components if we are to trust another person. Actions, rather than words, lead to trust. A lack of trust leads to insecurity, which in turn leads to stress, anxiety and low self-esteem.

In order to become a stress-free flyer we need to:
• build and restore our confidence so that we can regain a firm trust and a feeling of certainty in regards to flying,
• learn to let go of the need to control and begin to accept things and situations over which we feel we have no control
• learn to take each moment as it comes and to live in the present.

When we develop our fears about flying, we lose trust in two things. The first is the process of flying. We do not trust the judgement and decisions of the pilot and crew, the mechanical and technical worthiness of the aircraft, and the competence of the maintenance crew and air traffic controllers. Secondly, and most importantly, we lose trust and confidence in ourselves. Emerson said, "self trust is the first secret of success." We no longer believe that we can cope with the anxiety that may occur, or the emotional aspect of the fear. Our thoughts become immature and irrational, and our logic, at least in regard to flying, disappears.

Not only do we not trust ourselves with our feelings, but we do not trust others with them either. In fact, this lack of trust becomes generalized, and directed toward the flight crew and the actual aircraft so that we do not trust them with our *physical* selves. We transfer our focus from our intangible feelings and emotions to the tangible plane and the people who fly it. In other words, it makes far more sense to the fearful flyer, to admit that they are terrified of the aircraft or of the flight procedures than it is to admit to their *real* fear, which is of the feelings and the emotions which will surface when confronting an aeronautical experience. They can say that they hate to fly, hate planes, hate take-offs or landings, but seldom do they admit that they really hate themselves for the way that they feel under these circumstances. More importantly, they don't trust themselves or others with these feelings. Besides, if we have to confess to our fears at all, it is much safer and easier to explain our fear of being killed or physically hurt, than our fear of being emotionally hurt and exposed.

Our distrust tends to make us intolerant. Therefore, we do not give others a fair chance because we prejudge and always anticipate the worst in other people.

Distrust is usually the result of being misled. The distrustful person has always been let down and hurt in some way. It may be a case of having one's feelings discounted, or having been ridiculed, or rejected at some time. Distrustful people usually feel vulnerable and are always suspicious. The deeper the hurt, the deeper the mistrust.

The only way to eliminate fear and distrust is to learn to take risks and chances, both emotionally and physically. We take a risk and a chance when we fly just as we do when we reach out to trust another human being.

Risking is stressful. There are no absolutes, no guarantees, no certainties. To take a risk implies feeling out of control with regard to the outcome of the gamble.

In order to overcome our fear of flying we must be will

ing to take a risk and a chance. The restoration of confidence comes with the restoration of trust. There can be no trust without a level of risking. When trust is revitalized it promotes a healthier attitude.

Trusting the Captain and Crew

If you owned your own plane and could fly it, you wouldn't need to hire a plane and a licensed pilot. Unfortunately, few of us are in this position, so we use planes in the same way as taxis, buses and trains.

An airline captain and crew are well qualified and hand-selected for their positions. They love their careers, and look forward to promotions, raises and happy retirements just like anyone else. They have spouses, children, lovers, friends and families who count on them and need them. A pilot's job is highly coveted, and he or she is aware of its importance, and will work hard to maintain it. A captain or pilot for a commercial airline is the *creme-de-la-creme* of the industry. Have faith in your pilot. It is important to believe that he is reliable and dependable in everything that he does. A pilot's job is to check, check and check again.

These days, many more women are becoming airline pilots, so it should be no surprise to hear a female voice coming from the cockpit. She will have undergone exactly the same training and screening and be every bit as competent as her male counterpart.

Your pilot will be carrying extremely valuable cargo on his plane, including himself. He, as much as any of his passengers, wants to arrive at his destination safe and sound. I once saw a documentary film on air safety. The narrator asked the pilot being interviewed to what extent he worried about his passengers. He replied, "I don't worry about them at all, but I do worry about *me. I* know that if I'm alright, they will be very safe also. By not worrying about them I can concentrate better on doing my job."

The ground crew who service your aircraft are also highly trained and qualified, as are the air traffic controllers who direct the traffic. Their work is checked and re-checked by many back-up systems. Have faith in them also. They, too, look forward to promotions and an increase in salary. They like to sleep soundly and with a clear conscience.

It would be foolish to deny that human beings are imperfect and that mistakes do, sometimes, occur. But in the airline industry, the numerous back up systems and sophistica-tion of the procedures help to ensure that any errors that may occur can be called and corrected immediately. Thus, the chances of a human error leading to a disaster are very remote.

In order to be a confident and stress-free flyer, it pays to adopt a more realistic attitude toward our eventual demise. Death is inevitable for us all, but it doesn't necessarily follow that simply because we have chosen air transportation as a means of getting to our destination, that that is the way it is going to happen.

Trust is a reliable antidote to fear, but the first thing we have to learn is to trust ourselves.

LETTING GO OF THE NEED FOR CONTROL

When fearful flyers are asked what not being in control means to them, the usual response is that they are afraid of making a fool of themselves in front of other people. They may fear that they may begin to cry because they are afraid or that they will display anger or displeasure, perhaps even to begin shaking or trembling with fear. They are afraid of overt signs of fear and emotion which are perceived by themselves as being uncontrollable and somehow wrong or weak. They are afraid that if they did begin to cry, scream, yell or shake, they may not be able to stop and would then feel completely out of control. Of course, if this did happen it would be terrible for them, be-cause people around them would witness this occurrence and know that our fearful flyer, in losing control, really does have these feelings and emotions. The need for utter control can be broken down into two categories:

1. The trust factor. (Do the pilot and crew really know what they are doing?), and:
2. The fear of displaying emotions in front of others.

People spend a lifetime trying to hide and deny their feel-ings. Usually, they can escape when the going gets tough. But for a fearful flyer, once sealed inside a plane, (i.e. when the door is closed until it is opened for exit at the destination), they are physically trapped. Trapped, that is along with a lot of other people who become judge and jury, bound to be alerted to any strange happenings such as someone crying. Once on the plane, we are indeed in tight quarters. We are also trapped with our feelings and emotions, which somehow seem to become stronger the more we realize that we have no physical means of escape. Flying is one of the five situations in which we might find ourselves from which we cannot physically escape. The others are being submerged in a submarine, incarceration in a prison or some other locked facility, being buried alive (an actual dread for many people), and being on board a ferry boat or ship.

Some people pursue utter control, believing that it will provide the peace of mind that they are looking for. However, control at this level is an illusion. Control means to have the power to give orders or to restrain something. It is a means of regulating. Not many people enjoy the feeling of not being in control of their own space or life. As mature adults, we should not only be in control of, but also be responsible for, our own lives all of the time. The need for utter control is an unhealthy kind of control. It is *controlling*. Often, controlling people try to control others through manipulation, using guilt and shaming. The more out of control they feel, the more desperately they need to have utter control. There is a big difference between being in control and being controlling.

Eliminating the need for utter control doesn't mean that you will fall apart at the seams. Utter control is not keeping you glued together, neither is it stopping the plane from turning upside down. We need to understand that utter control serves no purpose, it is an illusion. To give it up means that nothing will change other than possibly having more energy and less stress. In addition, flying will certainly become easier for you. Nobody enjoys the feeling of not being in control of their own life.

The most important point to remember about control is that no-one can take it away from us without our permission. We can fear being out of control but we have to release control before it can be given or taken away. Therefore, we do have ultimate control. In order to be a stress-free flyer, we must relinquish a certain amount of our control to the captain and crew.

Acceptance

Letting go of unhealthy control means to experience acceptance. Stress free flying on a commercial aircraft requires absolute acceptance of the situation.

Much stress in our lives is produced by trying to fight things that cannot be changed. In the words of Dr. Robert Eliot, a noted cardiologist, "If you can't fight and you can't flee - flow."

If we recognize that we cannot effect a change, at least in the immediate situation, and let it go at that, we will be practising the art of acceptance. There is no way that we, as passengers, can physically fly the plane. We must leave that to the experienced and capable pilot up front in the cockpit. If we can learn to flow when flying, to stop fighting the situation and to stop planning our escape, our stress level will reduce drastically and our logic will return. Acceptance in this instance means to let go, to defer to another who has more knowledge and expertise. It also means learning to trust a superb piece of man-made machinery.

Flowing means acceptance. Once we can accept, wonderful things begin to happen. A feeling of calm enters the body and mind, and our fears melt away. Resistance and doubt disappear, and we find a restored level of confidence.

In preparing for flying, you should be aware that this acceptance phenomenon will most likely occur at sometime during your flight. Once it happens, you may experience a high from the feeling of acceptance. It is a feeling that you will wish for in your daily life as well. While this feeling is accentuated by the intensity of the situation, you should also be able to experience a similar feeling whenever you feel acceptance in other situations that require a degree of letting go. Strangely enough, letting go of the need to control actually gives us more control over our lives. The difference is that the control we can then exercise is a healthy, productive control. As a result, we experience a feeling of satisfaction and well-being, which, in turn, feeds our self confidence.

We always grow as a result of letting go.

LIVING IN THE NOW

Living in the now means to live one moment at a time and to live only in that very moment. To experience and enjoy what each moment has to offer.

As I have noted earlier, it is our thoughts that produce stress, not the stressor itself. It is what the fearful flyer *thinks* about flying that creates the fear, not the actual flying experience itself. Fearful flyers are good at projecting their minds forward into the future and thinking negatively about it.

"Living in the now" does not permit projected thinking. By living only in the present moment we can concentrate on the job at hand and remain calm, centred and in control of ourselves at all times. Our flying experiences will become far more successful.

Staying in the now keeps us focused on the present moment, the one in which we are actually living. After all, we can only be absolutely certain of this particular moment. We cannot deny the reality of the present or of life itself. It is when our imaginations take over that we run into trouble. To live in the future is to live in our imaginations, not in reality. Reality is now. If we stay in the now we can not be worried or anxious about future events.

When we fly, it is essential to take a moment at a time and then to live each moment in the now. We must think in terms of, "I am fine at this moment. Everything is O.K. right now. At this moment I am calm. Everything is under control and as it should be." Living in the now is a healthy circle of thought. (See Figure 2, page 64)

It is good to be optimistic and hopeful about the future. We all need goals, structure and objectives in our lives, things to work towards and to look forward to. This is our reason to live, our motivation. Optimism is healthy and quite different from projected thinking. For a fearful flyer, projected thinking is nearly always irrational, immature and catastrophic, the birthplace of fear.

To become a confident and successful flyer we need to learn how to live and enjoy the now, the present moment and not permit ourselves to worry about, or project our minds and our selves into, the future. The future will take care of itself.

The Healthy Circle of Living in the now

Healthy, mature and rational thoughts promote
healthy actions and reactions.

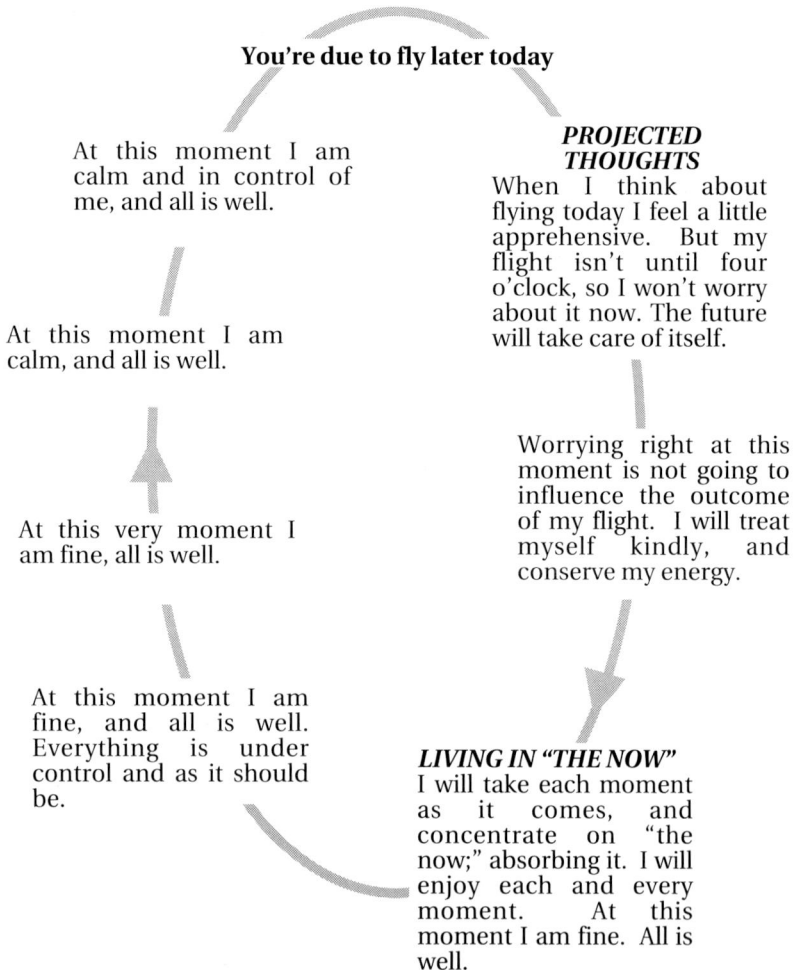

You're due to fly later today

At this moment I am calm and in control of me, and all is well.

At this moment I am calm, and all is well.

At this very moment I am fine, all is well.

At this moment I am fine, and all is well. Everything is under control and as it should be.

PROJECTED THOUGHTS
When I think about flying today I feel a little apprehensive. But my flight isn't until four o'clock, so I won't worry about it now. The future will take care of itself.

Worrying right at this moment is not going to influence the outcome of my flight. I will treat myself kindly, and conserve my energy.

LIVING IN "THE NOW"
I will take each moment as it comes, and concentrate on "the now;" absorbing it. I will enjoy each and every moment. At this moment I am fine. All is well.

Figure 2

CHAPTER NINE

The Support Person

"Tis not enough to help the feeble up, but to support him after."

Shakespeare (Timon of Athens)

T rying to explain a fear of flying can be difficult and stressful. Because the fear is irrational, it is out of proportion to the actual danger of the situation. Often, other people react with platitudes like "don't be silly," or "pull yourself together, there's nothing to be afraid of" (which is to discount the feelings of the flyer). Even the old cliche "it is safer to fly than it is to drive to the airport," is of little value to the fearful flyer. To them, the fear is real.

Jennifer, who had a fear of flying, was having difficulty in getting her husband and support person, Ian, to understand the magnitude of her fear. However, she knew that Ian was, himself, afraid of spiders. She asked her husband how he would feel if he were to be locked in a cupboard full of spiders for several hours. He shuddered and said that he would hate it, and that he would be so afraid that he might even go crazy. Jennifer replied that his dread of being locked away with spiders was the same feeling that she experienced whenever she had to fly. Ian understood when it was expressed to him in this way and he soon became more supportive and understanding of her fear.

It is difficult to describe the terror of a fear of flying, or indeed of any phobia, to those who have not experienced its pain in the same way.

CHOOSING YOUR SUPPORT PERSON

Not everybody can be a support person. It is a position that is earned. But a supporter can be a spouse, parent, friend,

lover, brother or sister, child, grandparent, in-law, cousin, co-worker, or even a flight attendant. Your supporter should be selected very carefully, as it has to be a person in whom you can have implicit trust. The other requirements for your support person are someone who:
• is dependable and predictable; someone you can really count on,
• is not going to embarrass you in any way,
• is on your side,
• is not judgemental,
• is not condescending,
• is patient
• is empathic
• does not discount your feelings,
• is calm, and not fearful themselves,
• tries to be understanding,
• is tolerant of your anxieties and concerns,
• is a good communicator.

It must be someone with whom you feel you can connect, and can leave feeling satisfied, listened to and taken seriously.

Finding someone with all of these qualities may well be a tall order. However, finding someone who fits most of them will probably be enough. You will know instinctively when the person you choose is right for you. It goes without saying, of course, that any such arrangement will have to be acceptable to both parties.

Participants in my fearful flyer groups are asked to complete a Trust Scale. This shows the amount of trust that each person has in their supporter. Many of them are horrified to learn that they have been using support people whom they simply do not trust. This lack of trust then adds to their anxiety while flying. It is vitally important that trust be your main ingredient when choosing a support person.

It may well be that while you don't really trust your spouse because you feel they don't understand your fears, you are obliged to travel with them. In these circumstances a flight attendant can serve as an excellent surrogate support person. Flight attendants may not be available to you every moment of your flight, but it can be a comfort to know that they are there for you if you need them. For fearful flyers travelling alone, this is especially useful. Being able to confide and put your trust in a flight attendant, and use them as your surrogate supporter can, and will, ease your anxiety considerably. All it takes is a little assertion. As you board the plane, mention to the purser or the attendant at the door that you are a fearful flyer and that you'd like to know that someone in charge is aware of your fears. They will make a note of your request and you will be monitored gently throughout the flight. There will be no big scene and nobody will embarrass you. From time to time they may ask you how you're doing. If they're not too busy they may spend time with you and chat for a while. If you need them urgently, you can simply push the call button on your seat and the attendant will head straight to your side.

My client Greg describes his first flight after his counselling this way. "On my inaugural flight I was put at ease by a wonderful flight attendant and an equally compassionate person sitting beside me. Upon boarding the plane I told them that I was a fearful flyer and that I would appreciate anything that they could do for me. Prior to take-off the flight attendant came back to me and, quite genuinely, inquired how I was doing. We talked for a bit and she told me that she'd be back right after take-off. She did return and she knelt beside me in the aisle. We talked at length about flying. She asked if I would like to talk to the pilots and she went up front to clear it with them first. While she was away I had an understanding conversation with the person beside me about the fear of flying. Shortly afterwards, we went up to the cockpit and I had a good conversation with the two pilots, who explained their navigational system to me. One of my biggest comforts is the realization that the pilot wants to get there safely as well."

Many people use flight attendants as surrogate support persons. It is a system that works easily and efficiently. Crew members who have to return to their home base, or to pick up another flight, are frequently given seats on flights as passengers. Quite often, when the flight attendants are aware that a passenger is nervous, they will place one of these crew members beside them. In this way they can be there for the nervous flyer, to talk to them if needed, explain engine sounds and flight procedures, escort them to the cockpit and share the occasional joke. If you can't count on your flying partner to fill the role of supporter, consider trusting flight personnel. They are usually only too happy to oblige. If you do not feel comfortable asking the purser as you board the plane, take a minute as you seat yourself and look for an attendant whom you feel you could trust. You must be assertive. Flight attendants are human too. Occasionally, you may meet one who is having a bad day and may not appear to be too interested in you or your phobia. If this should occur, contact the airline and report any negative experiences. The airline will thank you. They want you to continue flying with them. Your feedback helps them to maintain good service and high standards. They do not want to lose you to the competition!

HOW TO TREAT YOUR SUPPORT PERSON

With respect and gratitude! Never be demanding, whiny, pouty, obnoxious, belligerent or rude. Just because you have a fear doesn't give you license to be a general pain!

Consider yourself lucky if you have found the perfect supporter. They are to be treasured, not abused. Remember that you may have selected them, but that doesn't mean that they can't back away if they feel they are being taken advantage of. Most fearful flyers are so grateful to have a decent person sitting next to them that they will be eternally grateful. Kindness is always remembered.

THE SUPPORT PERSON OR SUPPORTER

A support person is someone who is ready, willing and able to assist a fearful flyer by providing them with strength and moral support. They are there to assist; to act as a mainstay, a Rock of Gibraltar, and an ongoing cheering section. The role of supporter means to give strength and encouragement to the fearful flyer as they embark on the road to recovery by facing their fears. To actually step back onto a plane after having been traumatized takes a great deal of courage.

There is a big difference between supporting and enabling. An enabler is one who supports through controlling and by making themselves indispensable. In the process they also allow themselves to be controlled. This is unhealthy support. Healthy support means to sustain another with no strings attached, no motives or hidden agendas. It means wanting, for the fearful flyer, only what they want for themselves - to be free from their fears.

Being the supporter of a fearful flyer should not mean a life-long undertaking. Rather, it should be looked upon as a short term commitment. Your phobic friend should be aiming for independence, to be able to fly without anxiety, and eventually without the aid of the support person. The job of the supporter is simply to be there for the fearful flyer, as they rebuild their confidence and change their attitude. It is rather like teaching someone to ride a bicycle. Sooner or later the trainer must let go of the bike and let the rider pedal on by themselves.

If the supporter does not let go at an appropriate time, they may well end up feeling trapped and used, and apprehensive about disengaging their services from the fearful flyer. This can lead to resentment on both sides.

A supporter may be enlisted for just one flight or for several. The fearful flyer, if well motivated, will be eager to test their own wings by flying solo as soon as possible, or at least ready to shift their role from that of a needy fearful flyer to a normal flyer, at which time the supporter will be relieved of their duties. In return, they will gain a calm and confident travelling companion.

Not all fearful flyers want or need a support person. The people who need support most are those who suffer from, or fear, loneliness, and those who have received little or no emotional support in their lives. The overly independent type may be happier left to their own devices. Some people simply cannot ask for help. In these cases, it doesn't hurt to offer your support anyway. Others are simply stubborn and resistant to what they consider any form of control. If you know of such a fearful flyer, there is no need to feel frustrated or rejected. You can still provide a cheering section from the ground.

Playing the role of supporter is not something that should be entered into lightly. It is a very responsible job. The supporter is accountable for the fearful flyer, no matter what happens, for it is the supporter that they will turn to for understanding, affirmation and support should they feel insecure.

The commitment to be a support person has to be one hundred and ten percent, and the role runs from the planning stage of the journey right up to the very end. It follows that, as a supporter, your trustworthiness is essential.

As a support person, it is just as important that you know what your fearful flyer needs and expects from you. The only way to find this out is by asking them directly. If you feel you are not the one for the job, that you can't handle it or simply don't need the added responsibility, then you must say so. Do not commit yourself and then let the fearful flyer down. You too, must be assertive. However, if you should accept the job, here are a few guidelines:

• You have been chosen as a supporter because your fearful flyer trusts you. Do not break that trust. Be predictable and dependable. If you say that you're going to do something, or

be somewhere, at a certain place or time then follow through. Do not let your phobic friend down at this crucial time. Emphasize that they can count on you, no matter what.
• Do not be judgemental, condescending, cynical or sarcastic.
• Try to be patient and tolerant. (The fearful flyer's introspection will be short lived.)
• Try to really understand your partner's fears, worries and concerns. Be empathic.
• Do not make fun of them or cause them any kind of embarrassment.
• Do not push. A little friendly persuasion sometimes works, but do not push your fearful flyer beyond their limits.
• Do not assume anything, always clarify.
• Be assertive with your fearful flyer.
• Communicate as openly as possible.
• Be a good listener.
• Encourage the fearful flyer to tell you when they feel anxious and when the anxiety has subsided so that you can understand what is going on.
• Do not discount their feelings.
• Be generous with encouragement and praise.
• Be a relaxed and good role model.
• Don't expect yourself to be perfect.

The fearful flyer's mood swings

Often, when people are fearful, they become frustrated and will act out in anger because they cannot say how afraid they really are. You also need to understand that quite often the fearful flyer's moods may swing when under the pressure of flying. They may become short-tempered, distant, cool, quiet, withdrawn, irritable, impatient, bossy or jumpy prior to or during the flight. You must try to see this as part of their fear. Often, the support person will see this change in behaviour and become defensive to it. The last thing we want for our fearful flyer is conflict. Once they settle down and accept their aeronautical experience, they will return to their old selves again. It's not easy being a fearful flyer, and sometimes the role of support person isn't easy either. But watching someone you deeply care for conquer an incapacitating fear can be very rewarding indeed.

A support person deserves praise and recognition for their valuable role and contribution to the success of the ex-fearful flyer.

Communication is the key

While I have talked about trust being the most important ingredient in a support person/fearful flyer relationship, the key once again lies in communication. The fearful flyer must feel comfortable enough with their supporter to be able to ask for anything that they might need done or said that is going to help them to settle down and relax and, hopefully, to enjoy their flight.

When preparing a fearful flyer for an upcoming flight, I usually request that the support person attend the session as well. In that way we can iron out any wrinkles or misconceptions and lay the ground rules for honest and open communication during the flight process.

Key phrases

I always ask the fearful flyer what it is that they need to hear if they're feeling a little edgy. Everyone has a key phrase that they find calming. Phrases like, "you're doing fine," or "just stay calm, you'll be alright," or, "everything's going well," are invaluable. Usually all the fearful flyer needs to know is that the support person will offer them their key phrase when, and if, they need it. No lectures, no advice or logic, just those important words. Of course, normal conversation will continue on and off throughout the flight. Sometimes the flyer will need their hand held or an arm to hold or squeeze. Overuse of Key Phrases can cause stress too. It is important that the fearful flyer convey the Key Phrase and any other requests prior to the flight so that the support person is fully aware of them ahead of time.

It may seem uncomfortable or foreign to the supporter to have to parrot a certain phrase to their fearful flyer. Remember that it is all part of your agreement to serve as an active supporter. It may seem stupid and meaningless to you, especially if it has to be requested and rehearsed. But the delivery of a particular phrase at a crucial moment may well be the most valuable thing you will ever do for your fearful flyer.

Sometimes the fearful flyer will ask for reassurance by asking questions such as, "I'm going to be alright aren't I?" or "Do you think the plane is safe?" Do not placate, but answer the question in a positive and confident manner. Eventually, we want the fearful flyer to be able to reassure themselves with the use of rational thinking and by staying calm and relaxed.

Assumption

Assumption can be one of the biggest mistakes in effective communication. Assumptions can, and often do, get us into a lot of trouble. Neither the supporter nor the fearful flyer are mind readers and no one should try to be one. At this point in recovery it is of the utmost importance that communication be open and honest on both sides.

If the fearful flyer does not want the support person to speak to them at all until spoken to, then honour it. They will come around when they are feeling less up tight. Everyone handles their stress and anxieties differently, that is why it is very important for the supporter to understand what the fearful flyer needs.

Alternative Plans

As you and your fearful flyer make your plans for your trip, it is always a good idea to prepare alternate plans for use in the event that they may have a change of heart at the last moment.

Alternative plans usually give the fearful flyer a feeling of healthy control, in that they do not feel completely pressured to go through with the flight if they feel it is premature.

I always suggest a backup plan to my clients when they are still a little hesitant about flying. We call it Plan B.

Plan A refers to the regular arrangements that you make for your trip, like the date, time, destination, etc.

Plan B is designed for the possibility that, if Plan A should be aborted, it is an alternative plan. For example, if you have planned a ski trip in the Rockies and your fearful flyer just can't get on that plane, you will be left with the decision of whether to go alone or to abort the flight. This is something very personal that the two of you would have to discuss and plan openly and honestly when you are in the early stages of planning your trip. It is important for the fearful flyer to have alternative plans in place early.

Plan B offers its own alternatives. For example, if your fearful flyer aborts Plan A, they may be able to compromise by driving or taking the train or bus to the mountains. They would travel alone, promising to meet up with you in a day or so. This would free you to continue on with your flight as originally planned and would allow the fearful flyer to have a shorter vacation without the guilt of having spoiled your holiday as well.

Alternatively, they may decide not to go at all, in which case you would be free either to carry on by yourself or to abort. This choice should be yours and then mutually agreed upon.

If your fearful flyer did decide to choose Plan B, they must make that decision with as little guilt as possible. Do not make it difficult for them. They will have a hard enough time dealing with their own frustrations, anger, disappointment and guilt should they decide to abort Plan A. They should be responsible for their own decision and its consequences, without making life miserable for you too. For the fearful flyer just knowing that they do have choices and that no one is pressuring them or making them do something they would prefer not to do, makes a huge difference to their attitude towards getting on that plane. They can always say to themselves that they don't have to do anything that they don't want to do. This is so freeing for them. Once they realize that the only thing they will lose is the price of their ticket, it really doesn't sound that bad. They do not have to lose either their pride or their confidence. It is no one's business but their own. As a matter of fact, they should be complimented for making their decision.

You may feel that the idea of having a Plan B is somewhat negative. However, if you can see it as an insurance then the chances are good that it will never be put into action. Of all the fearful flyers I have counselled over the years, not one has yet had to use Plan B other than as a comforting and empowering thought.

Weaning

To wean means to cause a person to gradually give up a habit. With the fearful flyer, this does not necessarily mean that you fly with them on one trip and not the next, unless, of course, there is a very good reason or they are ready to fly solo.

It is difficult, sometimes, to know when to begin the weaning process. It is probably best to take your lead from the fearful flyer. Most will be honest in terms of letting go. Premature weaning can cause setbacks. A setback means a regression or backslide in progress and, as we are trying to instill confidence in the fearful flyer, it follows that setbacks should be avoided. If in doubt, talk with your partner about it. If a therapist is involved, then by all means have a joint session to discuss the matter.

First of all, in order to wean, we must commence the process in the most comfortable and intelligent way, gradually reducing your role as caretaker one step at a time. This does not mean that you stop caring, communicating or encouraging. It means you gradually and slowly absolve yourself of the responsibility for the fearful flyer. The ultimate for them is to regain their confidence and, in doing so, reclaiming their independence.

Steps to take in the weaning process:

1. As you feel your fearful flyer becoming a little more confident, suggest that they take an active role in preparing for the next trip, such as making reservations and collecting tickets. Help them to stop avoiding flight preparation. Talk about the upcoming trip.
2. Take your lead from the fearful flyer. If you feel they need more independence, step back a little and give them more room.
3. As you feel them becoming even more confident, suggest that you sit in a different row of seats to the fearful flyer on the next trip.
4. Use the phrase nervous flyer rather than fearful flyer, when referring to your partner's fears. It implies more nervousness than anxiety.
5. Arrange to sit further apart from your partner if they want to experience independent flying, making the gap wider each time. Not everyone aims for independent flying, but it is a good idea. You may not always be available when they want to fly, or more importantly, have to fly.
6. Always remember the Key Phrases, even though you may not need to use them as frequently. When your partner no longer requires them from you, you will know that your stressful flyer is becoming a normal flyer and your job of supporter is near completion.
7. Celebrate any accomplishment together, no matter how big or how small.
8. Encourage a solo flight as a graduation.
9. Always be interested in and supportive of your partner when they fly, either with or without you.

LITTLE THINGS MEAN A LOT

A client, Joyce B., took her first flight after having received therapy for her fear of flying. Prior to therapy she was so nervous about flying that she had had to abort a long awaited retirement holiday in Hawaii, which she and her husband had planned. She told me, "there was no way that I could get on that plane, so two days before departure it was all cancelled with great feelings of guilt and disappointment."

Toward the end of her therapy Joyce asked her husband to be her supporter and together they took a successful eighty minute flight from Calgary to Vancouver. She even weathered some turbulence over the Rocky Mountains. After the flight, Joyce told me, "the moral support of my husband was an important factor. When we arrived back in Calgary I felt a great feeling of accomplishment and my husband surprised me completely by presenting me with a silver Indian Thunderbird bracelet upon landing. He said that he was so pleased and proud of me. I wear my bracelet every day to remind me that I can do it."

Yes, little things do mean a lot. I am not suggesting that by being a supporter you are required to shower your nervous flyer with gifts. But genuine words of praise, an affectionate hug or a kiss can certainly demonstrate just how pleased and proud you are of their accomplishments. And, of course, the nervous flyer can express their thanks to their supporter by a similar display of genuine feeling. Good friends are hard to come by.

CHAPTER TEN

All You Need To Do Is Relax!

"Relaxation is a gift that you can give yourself."

Anon.

Should you confess to your family or friends that you are a nervous or fearful flyer, frequently their reaction will be, "all you need to do is relax." True as that statement may be, implementation of their advice is easier said than done. Relaxation is a wonderful state to achieve, but you can only be totally relaxed when your mind, as well as your body, is relaxed and calm. It is your thoughts that cause the stress and tension for you. When you can let go of your stress and stressors and learn to read your stress warning signal your fears will begin to melt away.

If you truly want to fly with confidence and a healthy attitude, then you must learn the art of relaxation. It can be a wonderful tool for the nervous flyer and will help you to enjoy future flying experiences. Relaxation can also be applied to your daily life. It is a natural gift that we can give to ourselves. It promotes a happy and healthy way of life.

While you have had years of practice on how to become so tense, with a little training and practice you will be able to let go of unnecessary stress and tension in a surprisingly short time.

In our early years, many of us were neither encouraged or allowed to let go and just do nothing, to relax. Society dictated that no one should be idle. If we tried to do nothing we would be discouraged with guilt and shame. Relaxation was often referred to as being lazy. It would be implied that relaxing was unnecessary, if not downright undesirable. We were never taught the art of relaxation, or to relax without experiencing a level of guilt. But there are times in our lives when relaxation is not only earned and warranted, but is also crucial to our wellbeing. Relaxation increases our ability to endure stress and stressful situations, such as flying, and to remain calm in the face of life's pressures and difficulties. It permits us to focus, to concentrate and to feel more comfortable with ourselves.

Relaxation is the antithesis of anxiety and stress. In order to become a confident flyer we must learn the art of relaxation.

Relaxation is easy when you know how. It takes far less energy to be relaxed than it does to keep our tension alive. It is much more natural to be relaxed than to be tense.

People complain of not being able to make themselves relax, no matter how hard they try. The secret is to give yourself permission to relax and not to try to make yourself relax. Making yourself relax suggests an effort, which, in itself creates pressure and a certain level of stress. There is a big difference between allowing yourself to relax and making yourself relax.

There are two states we can choose to be in. The first is to be relaxed, the other is to be anxious. There is no in-between and we cannot be in both states at the same time. They are extreme opposites. But the choice is ours to make.

DO YOU HAVE A RELAXATION PHOBIA?

Some people are afraid to relax. They are so used to feeling uptight and knotted with tension that, should they ever begin to feel relaxed, they simply turn it off in favour of the more familiar feelings of anxiety. These people are fearful of anything that might help them to relax, from taking the occasional glass of wine to a tranquillizing agent. They will resist relaxation of any kind. The core of a relaxation phobia is the fear of losing control.

HOW DO I LEARN TO RELAX?

There are many ways to learn how to relax. One of the simplest is the do-it-yourself variety utilizing audio-cassette tapes. There are many different kinds of tapes on the market, providing spoken messages, music, or the soothing sounds of nature. Choosing a relaxation tape for you is a matter of personal choice. Some people find the sound of waves lapping on the shore soothing and pleasant, while others may find the same sounds irritating or distracting. You should find some tapes that suit your personality and needs. Make a collection of your own so that you don't become bored by using one tape repeatedly. You could make your own tape from your own favourite music or familiar comforting sounds. It is a good idea to select at least one spoken relaxation tape which guides you through the entire relaxation process, relaxing each muscle group, from head to toe.

For best effect you should get into the habit of using your tapes daily so that you can learn to identify the feelings of deep relaxation. The idea of relaxation therapy is to help you to become so proficient at relaxing that you will be able to produce it upon command, whenever and wherever you need a break from stress.

Some other effective methods of relaxation are meditation, yoga, Tai-Chi, a complete body massage, taking a sauna, a soak in a hot tub or a sudsy bath, or a brisk walk. The reason why the cassette tapes are so good is that they are portable. You can take a small cassette player on board the plane with you and you can listen to your tapes as you fly. It is difficult to tuck a hot-tub under your arm as you step onto the plane!

CORRECT BREATHING

Do not overlook proper breathing as an important part of the art of relaxation. We tend to think that because we breathe naturally and automatically from the moment of birth, we do not need to learn anything more about it. When we become tense and stressed our breathing is immediately affected. Under stress conditions, we either shallow breathe, which means we are breathing too fast and not deeply enough or we hyperventilate, which also means to breathe too quickly, but in this case moving too much air in and out of our lungs. In hyperventilation, there is an increase in the depth as well as the frequency of the breathing and the body is forced to receive excessive amounts of oxygen. It may seem difficult to take in enough air. It feels as though your chest just won't expand and you may even experience chest pains.

When you become aware of incorrect breathing, try sealing your lips tightly together, holding them with your fingers if necessary, to force yourself to breathe only through your nose. We tend to gulp air through our mouths when we are anxious. Because we are tense, we forget to exhale, or are too tense to let go of the breath. Do the above exercise for three minutes, or until your symptoms disappear.

Tense people tend to breathe from their upper chest area rather than from their abdominal region. The abdomen is where our natural breath should be released.

One of the very first steps towards relaxation is to learn how to stop the vicious cycle of anxiety by learning how to breathe correctly. Cassette tapes are also available to assist you with correct breathing techniques. They describe, step-by-step, how to take correct in and out breaths, a necessity for the art of relaxation.

LET'S GET PHYSICAL!

When you are flying, should you feel a little fidgety and restless, or if your body is beginning to feel stiff from sitting in one position for too long - get physical! Stimulate your circulation. There are simple exercises you can do while remaining in your seat that can help to get the blood flowing.

Moving your body periodically stops you from tensing and becoming taut or from locking your body into a fixed position. Moving or shifting your weight from time to time will help keep you flexible and more relaxed.

• Try gently shifting your body weight from one buttock to the other and then back again. Rocking and rolling from side to side a few times acts as a gentle massage. A numb rear-end is common to long distance travellers.
• Shrug your shoulders up to your ears, hold for a moment, then drop your shoulders down as far as they will go. Repeat a couple of times. This is a great tension reliever, especially for your shoulders and the back of your neck.
• Slowly and gently roll your head in a circle or from side to side, this will help to loosen your neck muscles.
• Stretch your fingers out until they feel stiff and then let them relax. Do the same with your toes. Stiffen and then relax. Repeat two or three times.
• Rotate your wrists, turning them first one way and then t h e other. Do the same with your ankles.
• Stretch your legs out as far as they will go, even if it is just an inch or so because of the seat in front of you. This will help to relieve any cramping in your knees and legs.

* NOTE (These exercises should not be done if you feel they will jeopardize your health in any way.)

Stretching is a great way to start relaxing your body. Tension will definitely constrict your body and sitting in one position for an extended period of time will give you a cramped feeling.

If you're really brave, you could take a walk in the aisle for a moment or two. Don't get run over by the flight attendants trolley though!

YOU ARE WHAT YOU WEAR!

A tip to enhance relaxation while flying is to dress sensibly. Choose loose, comfortable clothing. It is difficult to feel relaxed if your top button and your tie are blocking your airway, or your pantyhose are strangling you! Make your personal comfort a priority when travelling. Sometimes you see women boarding the plane wearing delicate dresses or suits and even hats. I often wonder if at the end of their journey they have managed to maintain that fresh appearance. It would be very difficult to relax dressed like this, especially if you worry about creases and stains or runs in your dainty hose.

Naturally, there are times when people have to be dressed appropriately for their destination. The executive who is flying into town for a meeting and heads straight for the boardroom may have no time to change clothing en route. It wouldn't look good if he or she walked into a high profile, formal meeting, wearing jeans and runners, even though this casual choice of clothing might have been more comfortable for the journey.

If you wear contact lenses, it is a good idea not to wear them while flying as the air in the plane tends to become very dry. After a while your eyes may become irritated if you keep your contacts in. The irritation would cause discomfort and elicit tension. Remove restricting belts, ties, scarves or jewellery. Be smart and don't wear tight fitting shoes, as sometimes our feet swell when we're up in the air. Try to keep your apparel loose for total comfort.

Think of all the things you can do to help make your flight stress free and as relaxed and comfortable as possible.

CHAPTER ELEVEN

Health Concerns

"If you look like your passport photo, you're too sick to travel!"

Will Kommen.

PSYCHOSOMATIC OR PHYSIOLOGICAL? (Imagined or real)

Sometimes when a person is feeling anxious or nervous prior to a flight, they have difficulty in determining whether they are really sick or whether it is just their nerves. Whether they simply are inclined to worry about their health generally, or even if they are true hypochondriacs (a condition in which a person constantly imagines that he is ill), they have to contend with the dilemma of deciding whether their sickness is real or imaginary.

When we are stressed, physical changes occur in our bodies. If we focus all of our energy and attention onto our bodies, then it stands to reason that we will notice these changes. By over-reacting to them, we can put ourselves into a state of even higher anxiety, which only serves to make matters worse. By letting our imaginations run wild, we soon find ourselves running to the doctor or confining ourselves to bed. The hypochondriac will imagine that all kinds of dreaded diseases are battling it out in their body.

By focusing on our state of health we don't have to face our real problems. Worrying about our health - hypochondria, whether mild or wild -serves as yet another smoke-screen to prevent us from admitting our real fears and concerns, which in the case of the flight phobic are the upcoming flight and the emotions attached to it.

Physiological - (real)

Many people, when they are nervous, experience physical upsets like diarrhoea, vomiting, loss of appetite or an inability to eat. When this happens, due to the stress of flying, a condition known as hypoglycaemia can result. Hypoglycaemia is sometimes referred to as a sugar-drop. In hypoglycaemia, the body has lost a lot of its nutrients and the person actually goes into a state of shock. To compensate for the loss of nutrients, the heart rate can increase, blood pressure may elevate, and the person may become anxious and light-headed. They may exhibit many of the symptoms of an anxiety or panic attack, such as weakness, tremors, even a feeling of faintness. If a person becomes dehydrated, the chances are good that they will become mildly hypoglycaemic.

The body's response to hypoglycaemia and dehydration is as if it were going into shock. The body then reacts in order to counteract that shock. The condition will not be rectified until food, and especially fluids, are replenished. Non-carbonated, non-alcoholic drinks, fruit juices or plain mineral water are the best to replenish body fluids. Eating food containing complex carbohydrates, like bread, pasta or grain, rather than foods which are made from refined sugar, will help to return energy to the body. Hypoglycaemia is the result of the body being depleted of essential nutrients and can be experienced by anyone who uses up their energy supply faster than they can replace the required body fuel.

Hypoglycaemia and, especially, dehydration are real conditions and need to be taken seriously.

If you have a fever, are experiencing severe or constant diarrhoea or vomiting, have a sore throat, or any other abnormal symptoms, it is always best to consult a doctor before thinking of flying. It is a sensible thing to do, as there are some physical conditions with which a person should not fly without a doctor's consent.

Some of the conditions which should be checked out by a doctor before flying are:
• Ear infections. Any obstruction in the Eustachian Tube can cause an inability to equalize pressure which can result in ear damage caused by the changing pressure in the aircraft.
• Any ear conditions which cause an inability to equalize pressure, or nerve damage within the ear are likely to cause vertigo, such as Meniere's Syndrome.
• Uncontrolled hypertension.

- Unstable heart conditions.
- A bad cold or upper respiratory infection.
- Severe lung conditions or diseases which can be affected by the reduced oxygen in the plane.
- If a contagious disease is detected you would probably be prohibited from flying.
- Pregnancy is usually acceptable up to 7 1/2 months, but your airline will have their own policies. Flying has no physiological effect on either the mother or the baby, but the airlines do not want the problem of having a baby born during a flight!

We are more inclined to worry about the things we do not understand. That is why, if in doubt, check with your physician. Your doctor is there to assist you and you need never feel guilty about asking questions that are connected to your well-being. This is an important part of taking control of your own life and being responsible for yourself.

JET LAG

Jet lag happens as the result of travelling a long distance in a short period of time in a jet plane. It only occurs when we are rapidly thrust into a completely different time zone. Whether the time difference be one hour or twenty, we will experience a degree of jet lag once we exit the plane into the new time zone.

Physical symptoms

Jet lag can produce feelings of exhaustion, restlessness and/or general fatigue or weariness. It can also temporarily affect our ability to concentrate, our memory and our general performance.

The reason why

Each of us possesses an internal clock or a master clock which is our body's time-keeper. Our master clock takes it's cues from our environment, such as the level of daylight, the brightness of sunlight, and local clock time-of-day, intake of food, drugs or medication, work, exercise, and periods of personal interaction. Combined, these customs or rituals connect through hormonal mediators within our bodies, and they reinforce our sense of time and place. They synchronize our daily body rhythms, otherwise known as our circadian rhythms.

Jet lag occurs when we have to adjust not only our wristwatch to a new local time, but also our own daily body rhythms of sleeping, waking, digestion and elimination, on the basis of a new time and place. It is a major adjustment and until our body can adapt to the new time frame, jet lag will take it's toll. Your body will feel out of sync. Jet lag is real.

How long does jet lag last?

As we are all individuals, it seems as though we each adjust to it in our own way and in our own time. Researchers have determined that, on a trip that requires a five to eight hour time change, it could take an individual anywhere from two days to two weeks to thoroughly regulate their sleep patterns.

Studies also show that, for some reason, recovery from an east to west trip is anywhere from 30% to 50% faster than our recovery would be from a west to east trip. When travelling from Montreal to Los Angeles you would cross three different time zones and would lose three hours of time. It makes sense to expect jet lag after losing three hours of your day! If you flew in a north/south direction, say from Vancouver to Australia, not only would it put you into a different time zone but also into a different hemisphere. You would arrive tomorrow today! No wonder your body would become confused. It has been used to sleeping, eating and rising at a certain time in correspondence with the sun. Your internal clock will expect breakfast at it's normal time and to sleep at it's regular time.

The effects of jet lag vary according to our physical condition, and seem to be worse in people who are unfit, ill or elderly.

How does jet lag affect nervous flyers?

As I said earlier, when we are stressed and anxious our bodies secrete hormones and neurotransmitters that unsettle our bodies' rhythms. The more anxious we become, the less flexible we are in adapting to new situations such as a new time zone. As a result our bodies will have more difficulty adjusting to an entirely new schedule. Jet lag produces it's own stress and if we are nervous flyers it will, quite possibly, take us a little longer to adjust.

Now that we understand jet lag, how can we beat it?

The first thing to remember is that jet lag is inevitable and quite normal. Everyone who travels through different time zones, including pilots and other flight crew members, experiences it to some degree. Our bodies never get used to the sudden switch in time and the accompanying routine. It is an unnatural occurrence. We may as well accept jet lag as a part of jet travel. It really is nothing to be feared as our bodies have the magical ability to adjust to the drastic changes in their own way. It is more often seen as an inconvenience by most seasoned travellers.

Just about every frequent flyer has their own version of how to overcome jet lag. The remedies are as varied as the people themselves. When I interviewed flight crew members I discovered that each person deals with it in their own way. Some crew members nap before they fly in order to get a refreshing head start, while others just sweat it out. Personally, I prefer a catch-up snooze upon arrival. Some folks like to tough it out and stay awake until the locals turn in for the night. I know business people who can step off of the plane and head straight to their meetings or classrooms and get involved intellectually and socially as a way of fighting off their jet lag. Some researchers claim that you can ward off jet lag altogether with the use of a three day systematic desensitization programme prior to your flight. This incorporates the use of darkness and light and a special pre-flight and post-flight diet. This programme is supposed to work very well, especially for frequent flyers.

Some sensible advice from a flight attendant was:
- Try eating light meals prior to and during the flight. Special menus are available upon request.
- Drink plenty of water and juice during the flight. Keep your alcohol consumption to a minimum. Avoid tea or coffee.
- Sleep as much as possible.
- Set your watch ahead or back to the time zone of your destination before leaving. This helps you to adjust mentally to the new time.

I heard recently that one of the major drug companies is experimenting with a new drug that could eliminate the symptoms of jet lag. It will not be available for general use for some time yet, but it just may be the answer.

Dealing with jet lag is a personal choice and I think it is

up to the individual to do what feels right for them. The secret is to be sensible, to relax and make it as easy on yourself as possible.

EXHAUSTION

In terms of physical ailments, exhaustion is the number one culprit in putting a damper on travelling of any kind. Next in line are stomach upsets and then tension headaches.

When we are exhausted, we are depleted of strength and energy. We feel tired out and stressed. We can be physically exhausted or emotionally exhausted or both. It isn't difficult to see how we can soon become fatigued when travelling. Not only are there last minute preparations and details like packing to be seen to before we leave but we can sometimes experience airport hassles, lineups, baggage or customs delays and, of course, there's all of the excitement as well.

The actual travel time can also be tiring. As I have discussed earlier, there can be jet lag to contend with as well as boredom and the discomfort of having to sit in one spot, often in one position, for several hours at a time.

When you arrive at your destination jet lagged, you may be tempted to head off immediately to do the things that are the purpose of your trip. The mistake that many travellers make is to try to do too much too soon and in too short a time which, of course, compounds any exhaustion they may be experiencing. You can overcome your exhaustion very easily, simply by pacing yourself. Cat-naps can really help you get through. You often see weary travellers asleep on the floor in the airport, using their knapsacks or sleeping bags as pillows. These people are smart. They are using their spare time wisely and catching up on much needed rest. I realize that not everyone wants to sleep on the floor, but if you can doze it does revive you a little. Don't forget to keep one eye on your flight time so that you don't miss your plane.

It seems as though a certain amount of exhaustion is an inevitable part of travelling. It is what you do with it that is important. You can either accept it and deal with it sensibly and revive quickly or deny it and end up feeling tired, cranky and stressed for the whole trip. The choice is yours.

BOREDOM

On a recent flight, one of my clients was beginning to feel a little bored and edgy so he put one of his cassettes on his tape recorder and proceeded to write down the lyrics to one of the songs as he listened. He was delighted, because it was something he had wanted to do for a long time and had never got around to and it passed the time for him. Boredom is one of the biggest problems for many people when they fly, especially if they are nervous flyers, simply because there is too much time to think. On your next trip, take something interesting to do to fill in the spare time. Some people like to play cards or read books or magazine articles, others prefer to use a lap-top computer and work as they travel. Crossword puzzles and word teasers can challenge your mind. Don't forget to pack your tape recorder and cassettes. Listening to your favourite tapes, whether they be relaxation tapes, music or even stories, can engage your mind in a positive way.

There is always an airline magazine available in the seat pocket ahead of you and most airlines will provide you with daily newspapers and current magazines to read during your flight. They also provide packs for children, with colouring books, crayons and puzzles. On longer trips your airline will usually provide headsets for listening to music or watching the in-flight movie. Remember that boredom can be your enemy. Learn to view your involuntary spare time as a gift and use it wisely. Relaxing is a luxury in itself, but to have time to relax is even better.

CHAPTER TWELVE

What Will Be Will Be!

> "Its easy enough to be pleasant,
> When life flows along like a song.
> But the man worth while,
> Is the man who can smile
> When everything goes wrong."
>
> Anon.

ATTITUDE

Realistically, we have to understand that no two flights are the same and that the absolute majority of them are routine. One flight may be as smooth as silk, while another may be turbulent - we have no control over the environmental atmosphere. One landing might be as soft as a marshmallow and another might be very hard, as though the plane is landing on square wheels. Sometimes, there are flight delays due to inclement weather, volume of traffic or mechanical problems. But when it comes down to it, it is a question of our attitude as to how we handle these unexpected changes and inconveniences. The Boy Scout motto is "Be Prepared." If we can learn to be prepared when flying, we can handle any changes without getting frazzled and upset. Simply go with the flow.

When I travel, I always take along some emergency food such as plain cookies or crackers and candies because you never know when you might be delayed. You can usually find something to drink in an airport, but food is not always so easily available, especially if the airport is crowded or if it's late in the day. I throw in magazines that I haven't got around to reading. They can help to fill in some waiting time. People-watching can be fun and interesting too.

When plans change, people often change as well. They tend to become uptight and angry with the system. It is well to remember that any flight delay is out of your control and certainly not abnormal. If you're worried about missing a connecting flight, your airline will do its best to hook you up with the next scheduled flight. Providing, of course, that you are booked with a reliable airline that does have a next scheduled flight. Sometimes flights are bumped and sometimes passengers are bumped. It can be frustrating and annoying when this happens but it isn't the end of the world. Be aware that often when a flight is cancelled due to mechanical problems, the airline may be cancelling it because it hasn't sold enough tickets.

Lynne, a friend of mine, was flying home after a business trip. Her seat was bumped because the airline had overbooked, so she had to take the next flight. When she wearily boarded the plane and had seated herself, she realized that she had been placed next to a very famous person, one whom she greatly admired. Lynne said that she felt it was all meant to be, because if she had taken her scheduled flight she would have missed this wonderful opportunity - fate had taken a hand. She was delighted with her new travelling companion, who turned out to be most gracious, warm and interesting. Lynne's flight passed all too quickly, and she had made a new friend into the bargain.

FAITH

"Feed your faith, and your doubts will starve to death."

Anon.

Not only does faith denote a system of religious beliefs, it also means to trust and to have confidence. Not everyone is a devout church-goer or attached to any particular doctrine. But we can all have our version or vision of faith. Philosophers have been trying for centuries to understand the basic truths and principles of the universe and of life itself. Health and happiness are a part of life. Death is a part of life. Misfortune is a part of life also. Woody Allen once said, "I'm not afraid to die. I just don't want to be there when it happens." I'm sure we can all relate to his sentiments.

Things happen sometimes that we just don't understand or particularly like but we are told repeatedly that all things happen for a good reason. This does not mean, however, that just because we have chosen to fly, something terrible will happen to us as a result.

We have faith that, as we walk across the street obeying traffic rules, we will make it safely to the other side. We seldom question the idea of stepping into the car and driving to the shopping centre and back; we have faith in our own driving abilities and sense of direction. If you want to become a confident flyer and fly with a healthy attitude you must have a form of faith. If we truly believe in God or a higher power, an entity who does have the final say for each and every one of us, then we cannot fight or argue the outcome of things.

FATE OR DESTINY

"Who can control his fate?"

Shakespeare (Othello)

If faith is too strong a word for you, how about fate or destiny? Fate means what is destined to happen and destiny means things that happen to a person which are thought of as determined in advance by fate. Use whichever word that feels comfortable for you: faith, fate or destiny, but whichever way you choose to look at it they mean basically the same thing - *What will be will be!* To believe truly in this philosophy means the ultimate in giving up control. At the same time, it also means the secret to stress-free flying.

My client Pat sums it up this way: "I now understand that my fear of flying was due to a fear of dying. I did not want to leave this earth! I now know I gave up some tremendous holiday situations that I really did deserve. I believe now, as well, that you have to be a fatalist - if it is your time to go, you'll go, no matter where you are."

CHAPTER THIRTEEN

How To Fly With Confidence And A Healthy Attitude

Here is a review of some of the most valuable points and tips raised in this book. They can be used as a quick and easy reference and a good reminder for yourself when you do fly.

1. On the day of your flight, reaffirm that you really do want to take this trip. It is your choice to fly to-day and no-one else's.
2. When you have made your decision to fly, relax and accept it. Don't fight it. Remember, also, that you are allowed to change your mind without feeling guilt or shame.
3. Dress sensibly. Wear loose, comfortable clothing if possible. Remove contact lenses to eliminate eye irritation because of the dryness in the plane. Do not wear any belts, jewellery or shoes that feel restrictive. Comfort should be a priority.
4. When flying, boredom can be your enemy. Don't give your mind the opportunity to get into mischief! Keep it engaged in a positive way. Put some interesting things to do in your hand luggage.
5. Take along your tape recorder and some relaxation tapes. Try to stay as relaxed as possible by using your tapes.
6. It's okay to feel a little nervous. If you have butterflies, fluttery heart or sweaty palms - it's nerves. RELAX - that's as bad as it gets. Remember, many people are a bit nervous when flying simply because it isn't the kind of thing they do every day.
7. It's okay to feel excited. Flying can be a most exhilarating experience and fun too. Do not confuse the feelings of excitement with nervousness. You may well be more excited than nervous. Imagine that!
8. Choose a trustworthy person to be your supporter. Someone you can have confidence in. Appreciate them and treat

them with respect.

9. If you are flying with a support person, communicate your thoughts and feelings. Request key phrases as you need them. Communication is a valuable key. Keep talking to your supporter. Keep talking positively to your inner self.

10. Live in the now. Take a moment at a time. Do not project your mind into the future, the future will take care of itself. Living in the now will help you to stay focused on the present.

11. Deal with emotional situations as they occur. You cannot afford to procrastinate on confrontation. If you are angry with someone or at something try to resolve the issue by being assertive long before you head to the airport. If it cannot be dealt with now, then vow to put it right as soon as possible. It is important that you fly with as little stress and distress as possible. ELIMINATE STRESS should be your motto when flying.

12. Be assertive, both in your everyday life and especially when you fly. It is your right as a human being to express your thoughts, feelings and opinions. It is alright to speak up for yourself and to get your personal needs meet.

13. Get to know your stress warning signals. Listen to your body talk!

14. It is your *thoughts* that create your anxiety and stress so keep those thoughts positive.

15. There is *always* a reason for your anxiety, it doesn't just happen.

16. It is very important to know and understand your basic fear and to become realistic about yourself.

17. By refraining from worry and projected thinking you will eliminate any anticipatory anxiety. Stop catastrophizing and you will have more energy to spare.

18. Use the elastic band trick to help change negative thoughts into healthy ones.

19. Remember that we are more inclined to worry about the things we do not understand. That is why it is important to be knowledgeable about flying in general. Educate yourself about the whole flight procedure. Use the question and answer section provided in this book to help you understand more about flying.

20. You *are* in control of your thoughts, feelings and emotions. Own them. Do not overreact.

21. Remember, no-one can take control away from you without your permission. You do have ultimate control.

22. Generally, try to restore a good level of trust. When we fly it

is time to put our trust and faith into other human beings, those who are experts and are more knowledgeable about flying than we are. Let go of the need for utter control. Remember, it is an illusion. Replace it with acceptance and trust.

23. Remember, the pilot will carry a very valuable cargo on his plane and it starts with him. He, too, wants to arrive at your destination safe and sound.

24. Your Captain and crew are well qualified and have been hand-selected for their jobs. They love their careers and look forward to promotions, raises and happy retirements. They have spouses, children, lovers, friends and families who count on them and need them. A pilot's job is highly coveted. He/she is aware of their position and works hard to maintain it. Being a Captain for a commercial airline is the *"creme-de-la-creme"* of the industry. TRUST YOUR CAPTAIN AND CREW. Have confidence in them.

25. The ground crew who service the mechanics of your aircraft are well trained and are very qualified. Their work is checked and re-checked by a back-up system. TRUST THEM. They too, look forward to promotions and an increase in pay and like to sleep at night with a clear conscience.

26. It is of the utmost importance that you trust yourself. Have confidence in *you* by firmly believing in yourself.

27. If you would be happier knowing what is going on in the cockpit, be assertive and ask the flight attendant, early in your flight, if you could go forward to meet the Captain. Usually, they will be happy to oblige. Of course, the timing has to be right. The cockpit crew cannot spend time with anyone when they are busy but they would call you at a quieter time when they would be pleased to talk with you, especially if they know you are a nervous flyer. Don't be afraid to ask, it's all part of the service that you pay for.

28. Remember, flying without stress is all up to you and your general attitude toward it.

29. Stay calm and relaxed. Drop those shoulders at least another inch. Take a deep breath. Relax your body and relax your mind. Try to give yourself permission to enjoy the experience of flying. It just might work!

30. Stay tuned to your body and your health in general. If in doubt ask your physician.

31. Phone the departures information line prior to leaving for the airport. Be prepared for any changes in flight plans.

Accept changes as a part of everyday flying. It happens to the best of us. Be flexible. Try not to over react. Yes, it can be annoying and inconvenient, but it isn't the end of the world! Just go with the flow and accept the situation.

32. Remember, you CAN overcome your fear of flying. The choice is yours. Keep your attitude healthy.

33. Keep the faith. What will be will be!

34. You have chosen the most expensive phobia! A large part of the cure is to practice, practice, practice!

35. Now, congratulate yourself on how well you are doing to this point. Go on, give it a try!

HOW CAN YOU TELL WHEN YOU'RE CURED?

Joan came to see me some time ago for help with her fear of flying. At that time, whenever she had to fly anywhere, she would spend the entire flight immobilized with fear. She would sit rigidly upright, her eyes looking straight ahead. She would refuse to talk to or acknowledge anyone around her, including her husband. She would feel that she had to focus all her concentration on flying the plane, if they were to arrive at their destination safely.

Recently, I received a letter from Joan. In it she told me of her progress. "Out over the Pacific, almost half way to Hawaii," she said, "the captain announced that we would be turning back to Vancouver because he had lost an engine! I wasn't too happy to hear that news but I felt confident that he would know the right thing to do. And would you believe that I even found myself telling a couple of other people, who seemed quite worried, that we would be okay as there are still three engines left. Now my husband and I are building up air miles on our frequent flyer plan. So far we have had two free flights. I would never have believed that some day I would be chalking up air miles."

Another client, Chuck, recently sent me a postcard from Germany. "We had a perfect flight. Are the planes better now, or is it the pilots, or what? Flying is improved . . . or could it be me?"

But the most memorable came from Chris, following a trip to Toronto. "I have truly earned my wings," she said, "frankly, there isn't anything to fear in flying."

PART THREE

Be An Informed Flyer

Answers To Your Questions About Flying

I n order to fly without fear it is important to know as much as possible about the aircraft that you will be on, how it is operated and controlled and the measures that are taken to ensure the safety, comfort and well-being of the passengers. Fearful flyers, no matter how brave they may be about venturing onto an airplane, still have many questions about the whole process. The questions in this section represent some of the concerns about flying that I have found to be most frequently expressed by fearful flyers. The answers have been provided by professional pilots, flight attendants, air traffic controllers, doctors, nurses and other airline personnel.

Questions most frequently asked about the people who have control over your flight

QUESTIONS MOST FREQUENTLY ASKED ABOUT THE PEOPLE WHO HAVE CONTROL OVER YOUR FLIGHT

THE PILOT

How does one become a pilot?

There are a number of ways for a person to become an airline pilot but the best training ground for pilots is still the military. Service as a military pilot provides excellent training for commercial aviation and flyers from the Armed Forces have a better chance of being accepted for further training by the airlines. Not all pilots come from the military, however. There are a number of good flight training colleges throughout the country, as well as local flying clubs and flying schools, which can provide basic flight training. The Royal Canadian Air Cadets gives many teenagers an early start with glider pilot and private pilot scholarships. Many airline pilots began flying that way. And, of course, all of the airlines have their own extensive training programs for both new and experienced pilots.

What are the minimum and maximum ages for a pilot?

A person can obtain a pilot's license at age sixteen. An airline would probably not hire a pilot of that age, simply because he or she wouldn't have accumulated enough flying experience. Normally, airline pilots start in their mid-twenties, providing they have the required background, qualifications and experience. Retirement ages differ between companies, but most of the major airlines make their pilots retire at age sixty. Smaller airlines may allow their pilots to fly up to age sixty-five. Remember, though, that all pilots must pass a rigorous physical and mental examination each year; after the age of 40, this is required every six months and any pilot who cannot meet the requirements of this test will be retired, no matter what their age.

What about a pilot's health? Who decides whether a pilot will fly if he is not feeling well?

Basically, the decision whether or not to fly rests with the pilot himself. He must book off sick if he is not feeling up to par. He certainly wouldn't fly if he was suffering with a cold or the flu, because of the possibility of damage to his ears from the changes in pressure. If a pilot is sick, he must check with the airline's doctor who can, if necessary, prevent him from flying while using certain medications or until his condition improves. He will then have to see the doctor again and get his permission before returning to flight duties.

Do pilots have a regular medical and psychological check-up?

Yes, they do. All pilots are required to undergo a thorough medical checkup at least once a year. Any pilot over the age of forty has a total of five checkups over a two year period - one every six months, plus a very extensive checkup at least once in any two year period. These checkups include physical and laboratory testing, as well as investigation of the pilot's personal life, such as drinking habits, smoking habits, psychological stress, etc. The doctor performing the checkups can ground a pilot for any medical or psychological reason, and before that pilot would be allowed to fly again, he would have to undergo further testing to prove that the reason for the grounding no longer exists.

Is there a limit on how many hours a pilot can fly?

A pilot's flying hours are limited, both by Government regulation and by the collective agreement negotiated by the pilot's union. The limitation also differs according to the type of aircraft being flown as well as a restriction on the number of take-offs and landings that he can perform in any period.

How many take-offs and landings is a pilot permitted to make on each trip?

Take-offs and landings are stressful for the pilot and there are restrictions on the number that he can perform in any given period. There is no set number of take-offs and landings that can be performed on any one trip, but a pilot will be restricted in the number he can do in a month. On a large, wide-body jet, for instance, there is usually only one take off and landing per trip. Occasionally, on a very long flight, there may be more and, in that case, the take-off and landing procedures would be shared between all the pilots on board the flight. Remember, each member of the cockpit crew is a fully-qualified pilot trained to fly that particular plane.

Are there any prescription or over-the-counter drugs that must not be used by pilots when flying?

There are no set rules for this, but certainly a pilot should stay away from any drugs that may cause drowsiness or loss of concentration. There is a long list of specific medications that pilots cannot use while continuing to fly. Basically, these are any mood altering drugs, anti-depressants, anti-hypertensive medications, cardiac medications, narcotics, sedatives and muscle relaxants. Among non-prescription medications are analgesic or pain killers and anti-histamines which can cause drowsiness. A pilot using any of the prohibited medications is required to report the fact, and will be prevented from flying until he is re-certified by his company doctor.

What are the rules regarding alcohol and drug intake prior to flights? Are the crews checked for this prior to a flight, or are they on an honour system?

The use of drugs is absolutely forbidden, not only for a pilot, but for any member of a flight crew. Pilots are not allowed to use alcohol within twelve hours of a flight. Any breach of this rule results in instant dismissal

Who makes up a pilot's flight schedule?

Pilots are assigned flights by way of a bidding system. Each airline provides a list of flights for an upcoming period and the pilots bid, from these lists, for the flights that they want. Flight assignments are subject to the pilot's seniority, their qualification for the type of aircraft to be used, and other factors. They also bid for the type of plane they want to fly. Pilots can only fly one type of plane at a time and must re-qualify whenever they switch to another type.

How long before a flight must the pilot be in the terminal? What does he do during that time?

Normally all members of the flight crew are required to check in at least one hour before their flight time. This time is spent in flight planning, being briefed on weather conditions, checking on fuel requirements and other information. Further time is spent on board the aircraft doing pre-flight checks.

Question to a pilot - *"which do you enjoy more, driving your car or flying a plane?"*

"Flying a plane, by far. I can do a much better job flying than I can driving and it is much safer. I am always aware that the most inexperienced pilot is perhaps twenty times more qualified to fly a plane than anybody driving a car."

Why is it that sometimes the captain will come on the public address system or sometimes the first officer? Why do they do this at times and not others?

Whether or not the captain, or the pilot flying the plane makes announcements over the public address system, is pretty well up to the officers involved. Normally, on flights of less than one hour, all the pilots are too busy to make announcements. It takes about half an hour to get a plane up, and another half an hour to get it down again. Flights longer than one hour give the pilots a little more time, and they may, or may not, wish to say something to the passengers. Remember, that all the flight crew are trained pilots. Only one of them, not necessarily the captain, will be actually flying the plane at any time, so that if the first officer makes the announcements it means that the captain is flying the plane at that time. If the captain does it, then the first officer is flying, and so on.

Why do pilots sometimes walk through the plane during a flight? Don't they know that it terrifies some people to see them away from the controls?

Your pilot, or any other member of the flight crew, may sometimes walk through the passenger cabin. This may be for any number of reasons, not the least of which would be simply the need to stretch their legs after several hours of sitting in a somewhat cramped cockpit, or to use the washroom. They are aware that this makes some people uncomfortable, but you may be assured that if anything was wrong the pilot would be at his post, and not strolling calmly through the back of the plane. Remember that, besides the captain, there is always one, and often two, other highly trained and completely qualified pilots on board, one of whom will be in charge of flying the plane at any time. In fact, on very long flights, there may well be a complete relief crew which will take over the flying duty half way through the flight. In this case, one complete crew is off duty and why shouldn't they stroll through the plane from time to time?

What legal powers does the captain have?

Air captains can not marry people, as a ship's captain supposedly can. However, a pilot in charge of a plane is a peace officer with all the powers inherent in that responsibility, including the power of arrest. In fact, the captain has pretty well absolute authority over his plane and the passengers.

THE CABIN CREW

How does one become a flight attendant?

Generally, flight attendants are chosen on the basis of their inter-personal skills and experience in dealing with the public. The actual requirements for the job of flight attendant differ from airline to airline. However, one thing is common, a very intensive, hands-on training program of at least six weeks duration, which includes all aspects of flight service and safety. Candidates are given emergency training using the actual equipment found on an aircraft. Before going on a real flight, a trainee flight attendant is instructed in the operation of specific equipment and aircraft used by their airline. In Canada, every flight attendant must re-qualify by undergoing a refresher training course every year. This includes emergency training in an aircraft simulator.

Promotion within the airline is based on length of service, work record, and completion of training courses. Flight attendants compete for available positions at higher levels.

What are the duties of a flight attendant?

The main duties of a flight attendant are to ensure that passengers are afforded a high level of comfort and security, within the regulations under which the airline operates. While flight attendants appear to spend most or all of their time in serving their passengers, readiness and training for emergencies is the underlying and paramount duty of a flight attendant.

What are the duties of a supervisor?

There are two types of flight attendant supervisors. The "In-charge," (sometimes called the Purser), is the head attendant in charge of a particular flight. The In-charge flies with the flight attendants and supervises their duties. A supervisor is a ground based person who is responsible for the quality of service, training and duties of a number of flight attendants. A supervisor will occasionally come on board a flight to monitor the level of service, the adherence to safety regulations, training levels, and so on.

Are there any restrictions on how many hours flight attendants can fly in a day, a week, or a month?

The number of hours that flight attendants are permitted to fly varies with the type of duty they are doing and the airline that they work for. As an example, the following were provided by one of the major Canadian airlines: On domestic flights, operating out of a base where a full crew is located, a flight attendant could fly up to fourteen hours in a day. On an overseas flight, with an overnight stay before returning to base, they could fly up to sixteen hours in a day. Normally, flight attendants fly a minimum of sixty-five hours in a month, with a maximum flying time of eighty-five hours in a month.

Are flight attendants restricted in their use of alcohol and drugs?

Flight attendants are not permitted to drink alcohol within twelve hours of a flight departure, or within twelve hours of being on call for a flight. The use of narcotic drugs is, of course, strictly prohibited at any time. In addition, they are not permitted to use prescription or non-prescription drugs that may cause drowsiness or loss of attention, such as cold remedies or antihistamines. In addition to all that, flight attendants are not permitted to donate blood, except in emergency situations, or to go scuba diving, within twenty-four hours of a flight.

How long before a flight do flight attendants have to be in the terminal? What do they do before boarding the plane?

This depends on the type of aircraft being flown. The larger the aircraft, the longer the time before flight time that the crew has to report. This is usually about one hour. The crew will gather in the crew lounge, where they receive a service and safety briefing on the aircraft being used. At this time, also, any problems encountered on previous flights are discussed. Occasionally, they will practice for a hypothetical situation, like a passenger having a heart attack, or an evacuation. Generally, the cabin crew board the plane thirty to forty minutes before the flight, again, depending on the size of the plane. Once on board, they check all the emergency equipment, all the service equipment, the food, make sure that the washrooms work, and perform general housekeeping duties prior to the passengers coming on board.

Why do the attendants phone one another during the flight?

On a large plane, flight attendants can not always find one another readily when they need to communicate something. So they use the telephones. The telephones are also used to coordinate the duties of the many attendants on the flight. On a large plane, for example, watch the flight attendants while the plane is taxiing out to the runway. There will be a flight attendant on each telephone. They are going through a strict pre-take-off drill, confirming to the in-charge attendant that all safety procedures have been checked in their sections.

Why does the supervisor count passengers prior to take-off?

This is done for several reasons, among them the need to provide the pilot with an assessment of the approximate weight of the passengers that he has on board. This will affect the amount of cargo that can be carried. In addition, as a security measure, the number of people on board must equal the number who have checked in for the flight. Any discrepancy between these two numbers will be immediately investigated, and the plane will not take off until it is reconciled.

Why do the flight attendants go through their safety demonstration while taxiing? Do people really pay attention?

The demonstration of safety equipment and procedures is a government regulation in the United States, Canada and most other countries. While it may appear that nobody is listening, it must nevertheless be given each and every time that the plane takes off. In the newer planes the safety demonstration is given on a video screen. Flight attendants report that more people appear to pay attention to it this way.

What would the flight attendants do if a passenger became locked in the washroom? How would they know?

Many people are afraid of going into the washroom on a plane for this very reason. They are afraid that they may become trapped in there, and have to remain inside, undetected, throughout the entire flight, perhaps longer! First, the likelihood of this happening is quite remote. However, should it occur the doors to the washrooms are quite flimsy, and any knocking or shaking would soon be noticed by other passengers or the flight attendants. It is then a very simple procedure for them to open the door from the outside. The aircraft designers have already thought of this possible problem and the door mechanisms are designed to be opened in this way for that very purpose.

Flight attendants always appear to be so busy. What is the best time to talk to them about my fear of flying?

The best time to mention your fear of flying is when first boarding the plane. Mention it to the in-charge flight attendant. He or she will pass it along to the other flight attendants. You could also identify yourself to any of the flight attendants as they walk through the cabin, or when they are serving you with drinks or meals. Remember that flight attendants are constantly watching their passengers and they are trained to watch for symptoms of extreme nervousness. This is done, not only for the comfort of the passengers, but also in case an emergency situation should arise.

When is the busiest time for flight attendants, the time when they'd rather not be bothered by requests or questions?

The two times that flight attendants are simply too busy to attend to requests and questions from the passengers are just prior to take-off, and again just prior to landing. At these times the flight attendants perform what they call a silent review, when they go over a set of commands that must be repeated, mentally, during every take-off and every landing. This review covers such things as emergency procedures, what to do if something goes wrong and which passengers they have selected that may need special assistance in such a case.

What do the flight attendants do with rowdy passengers?

Occasionally, a passenger will become rowdy, either from having had too much to drink or perhaps just high spirits. Their behaviour may also be caused by nervousness. Flight attendants watch their passengers constantly and a chain of communication starts between the crew members the moment the passengers are on board. They note seat numbers of people who they feel may turn out to be troublesome and all crew members are made aware. They may decide to refuse drinks to a person who has obviously had enough. They watch potentially troublesome passengers, and try to head off any trouble before it gets started. Should a passenger become rowdy, and the flight attendants unable to control them, the captain would be informed. He can order a passenger to be restrained if necessary. If the situation warrants, he may land at the closest airport. In this case, he would radio ahead, the plane would be met by the police and the passenger would be arrested and charged. In such a situation the rowdy passenger would be obliged to pay the extra cost to the airline of the unscheduled landing and take-off.

Can the flight attendants put a limit on how many drinks a passenger can have?

Yes, they can. If the flight attendants feel that a passenger has been drinking heavily before boarding the plane, like a waiter in a restaurant they have the power to cut a passenger off before they start, They can also deny boarding to any passenger they feel is impaired or who may be a problem during the flight.

Is there a fully trained first aid person on every flight? What kind of training do they have?

All major airlines give their employees a general first aid course, which is usually taught at least once a year. The course examines common ailments that might be encountered on an airplane. It is not a requirement that a person trained in first aid be on every flight.

Quite often we notice that the pilot will signal for the flight

attendants. Why do they do this?

During a flight there may be any number of reasons for the pilot to talk to the flight attendants. They may wish to give instructions regarding meals, they may want a cup of coffee or they may have information to relate regarding scheduling, late arrival, upcoming turbulence, etc. There is no reason for concern just because the pilot summons the flight attendant to the cockpit.

What might a flight attendant do for a passenger if they told them that they were terrified of flying?

First, it is a good idea to mention your fear of flying to the airline agent prior to boarding the flight. This information would then be noted and relayed to the purser, and to every member of the cabin crew. The flight attendants working your section of the plane would then be able to monitor you throughout the flight. The flight attendants have a system whereby they make notes of such information, and your name and seat number would be posted in a crew area, so that everybody would be aware that you are nervous. Flight attendants will check on you periodically throughout the flight. They may be able to move you to a better seat if one is available. If it would help, they could arrange a visit to the cockpit for you. They can only do these things for you if they are aware that you need them.

Are the flight attendants aware that nervous flyers are constantly watching them for signs of nervousness or unease?

Most flight attendants are quite aware that the public are watching them. Rules regarding conduct and standards of behaviour are all laid down in company manuals and they are instructed in how to deal with all different types of people and situations that can arise.

Can flight attendants develop the fear of flying?

Flight phobia is not restricted to passengers. A phobia is an irrational fear and can occur in anybody at any time. There are instances of flight personnel, including flight attendants and even pilots, who have suddenly developed an irrational fear of flying for no discernible reason, sometimes after many years of safe flying.

What happens if someone should smoke in a washroom on a non-smoking flight?

All planes are equipped with sensitive smoke detectors, especially in the washrooms. Anyone smoking, or, worse, tampering with the smoke detector so as to be able to smoke, will immediately set off an alarm both in the flight attendant's area and in the cockpit. When this happens, the passenger will be asked to stop smoking immediately, and, quite possibly they will be reported to the police on landing where a charge could be laid against them.

What is the longest and the shortest destination stop-overs for flight attendants?

The longest stop-over can be two, three, or even four days, depending on the schedule. The shortest, under the terms of the union contract, must be no less than ten hours.

How long does a flight crew stay at a destination before returning to their home base?

When a crew has to stay at a remote destination before returning home, they are required, by law and the contract with their union, to stay at least eleven or twelve hours, depending on whether their hotel is near the airport or downtown. A stop-over can frequently be longer, sometimes a week or more.

THE MECHANICS

There always seem to be mechanics doing something to the plane when the passengers are getting ready to board. What do the mechanics do on the ground prior to a flight?

They do a number of things, depending on the time that the plane is on the ground between flights. For one thing, any minor problems with the aircraft, things that may not be working properly, but that do not affect the safety or performance of the plane, can be repaired at this time. For example, things like faulty washrooms, burned out light bulbs, or seats that are jammed. In addition, a senior mechanic always does a walk-around, that is, a visual check of the plane from the outside to spot any obvious problems that may affect safety and security. If he does, then the plane would be grounded and prevented from taking off until the problems are rectified. You may also notice one of the pilots doing a walk-around inspection as well.

How does a person become an aircraft mechanic?

There are several ways that a person can be trained to service aircraft. Most mechanics today are graduates either of the Armed Forces or one of the aircraft maintenance programs offered at many colleges across the country. After initial training, each airline and each aircraft manufacturer, provide further classroom and practical training on the actual aircraft used by their airline. Until certified as fully qualified, a mechanic is not allowed to work alone or to sign for work they may have done.

How many hours does an aircraft mechanic work each shift? How many days a week?

This differs from airline to airline, but, like most aspects of aviation, each airline must operate within strict standards laid down by government regulations. Generally, mechanics work regular forty hour weeks. Should they work more than this, they must have a minimum of eight hours off between shifts. In addition, regulations limit a mechanic from working more than a certain number of hours of overtime in any three month period.

How often does the plane get a thorough check-up?

Planes get checked out for mechanical efficiency on a regular basis to conform with standards set out for them by government regulations. Usually, a service check is performed on every aircraft every day. This takes approximately two hours and covers all the operating and safety equipment on the plane. Any defects will be repaired at that time. The plane will be grounded for a longer period if the job can not be completed during the check. Other checks, scheduled for every plane at regular intervals may take anywhere from one night up to a full month. To complete this may involve anywhere from thirty to as many as eighty people, working full time. A major check-up such as this would be performed on a routine basis approximately once every five years, depending on how many hours the plane has flown.

Is all the work of the mechanics double-checked?

Most work on an aircraft, other than very routine, minor repairs, is checked by another mechanic besides the one doing the work. Certainly, any work on the flight control systems, that is, the controls and mechanisms which actually operate the plane during flight, is checked and signed for by two qualified technicians. During the plane's major check-ups all work is verified by an inspector before the plane is certified to go back into service.

AIR TRAFFIC CONTROLLERS

What training is required to be an air traffic controller?

Potential air traffic controllers have to undergo a very rigorous selection and interview process, which includes extensive aptitude testing. Once selected, a candidate is sent to a government operated training institute for a course running for up to nine months. He/she would then probably be assigned to a smaller, outlying control tower for six to nine months for on-the-job training. They would then be licensed to control traffic at that smaller tower only. A licensed controller can bid for postings to larger centres, but even so, each new posting would involve further classroom and on-the-job training before their license would be endorsed for the new location. A controller moving from a small airport to a large city, for example, would be required to spend ten days in the classroom, a further thirty days in the tower working under another controller, then back into the classroom for ten more days. Even after that, they would have to spend four more months training on the job before they can be licensed to operate on their own in the large airport. That is a total of about nine months training each time a controller moves to a larger location. Even moving within their own area, such as moving from the tower into the radar room involves a sixteen week simulation course followed by another four months training on the new job. In addition, each year, every controller must go through a refresher training course of three to five days duration. They are also required, once every five years, to demonstrate their ability to take over and control traffic without the use of radar in case that should ever become necessary.

How old must a person be to become an air traffic controller? At what age do they retire?

Under the rules of the International Civil Aviation Organization, which governs civil aviation virtually throughout the world, a person must be at least twenty-one years of age before they can be registered as an air traffic controller. Normally, an operational controller, that is one actually working in air traffic control as opposed to an administrative position, can retire after the age of forty-five with twenty or more years of service. While there is no mandatory retirement age, each controller is required to pass the same aviation medical examination as a commercial pilot every year. Most air traffic controllers, like most pilots, tend to retire in their early fifties.

Is there a limit on how many hours an air traffic controller is allowed to work at one stretch? How many hours per week?

Generally speaking, air traffic controllers work shifts that are normally seven hours and can not exceed twelve hours, at a stretch. The normal work week is thirty-four hours. They take meal and relief breaks during their shifts, depending on how busy they are and on other operational requirements. Usually they receive three short breaks within each shift.

For any number of reasons, a person's concentration level can be down from time to time. How do air traffic controllers deal with this?

If personal problems are interfering with their level of concentration, a controller would be removed from his post until he could demonstrate his ability to function properly again. Air traffic controllers, like pilots, have the right, indeed they are obliged by law, not to work when they are sick, or if they are using any of a lengthy list of specified medications. Use of many over-the-counter medications, such as antihistamines, or most common cold remedies, will invalidate their annual medical examination and they will not be allowed to work again until they have been certified fit by a medical officer. The use of alcohol by a controller is restricted in the same way as for pilots. They can not work within eight hours of their last drink.

GENERAL QUESTIONS ABOUT THE CREW AND FLIGHT PROCEDURES

Should I keep my seatbelt buckled all of the time?

The seatbelts are there in case of a sudden stop, just like the seatbelts in your car. They are also there to restrain you in the event of turbulence or some sudden movement of the plane. For this reason airlines recommend that you keep the belt lightly buckled at all times while you are seated.

How many crew members are there in the cockpit and what are their duties?

This will depend on the plane, but there are always at least two, and sometimes three or four members of the flight crew. The captain is the aircraft commander. He has total responsibility for the plane, the passengers and the flight. The first officer is an assistant to the captain, and will take on the actual flying of the plane for at least part of the flight. A second officer will usually be a flight engineer responsible for the equipment on board; radio, radar and navigation. This officer would probably not do any actual flying but would be a fully qualified pilot capable of flying the plane if necessary.

Is the cockpit door always locked? Why?

This varies from country to country. United States law requires that, for security reasons, the door to the cockpit be locked at all times. In Canada, this is not the case, but access to the cockpit is restricted and you would not be allowed to enter unless accompanied by a member of the crew.

How do we know that the food being served is fresh?

The food on board is checked both at the time of boarding and before and during the heating process. Airline food is prepared with meticulous care and is kept refrigerated until it is re-heated on the plane. In addition, flight attendants taste-test samples of the food before it is served. In the event of a long delay in serving, due to flight delays, or whatever, any food on board the plane would be discarded and replaced with fresh food.

What method of cooking is used on board?

The food served on the plane is heated in electrical dry heat ovens. The food is partly cooked at the commissary, depending on the type of aircraft and the length of the flight. For example, food prepared for a very short flight of just an hour or so would be more thoroughly cooked on the ground than food for a long, overseas flight where there is plenty of time for thorough cooking on board. The type of food served also differs according to the length of the flight and the amount of cooking required.

Is it true that the pilot and first officer eat different meals to avoid food poisoning?

Yes. Flight regulations state that meals for the pilot and the first officer must be different from each other, cooked in different ovens and placed on board the flight separately from each other.

During the flight we often hear "binging" sounds. What are they and what do they mean?

These "bings", or chimes, are a communication system. There are a number of combinations of signals, all of which mean something to the crew. Perhaps the one that most passengers notice is the "three chimes" heard as the plane is taxiing out to the end of the runway. This means that the captain has received clearance for take off and is a signal for the flight attendants to prepare. The three chimes are also used when descending to instruct the flight attendants to prepare for landing. Other combinations of chimes are used to signal flight attendants for any number of reasons, either by passengers or by the flight crew.

Can a nervous passenger request a drink of water prior to take-off?

Certainly. Flight attendants will bring you a cup of water if you want one. There are also plastic water cups in the washrooms. You can visit the washrooms at any time prior to the time the plane is pushed back from the gate.

Is there any time while on the plane that I cannot use the washrooms?

Yes, you can not use the washrooms just prior to take off, while taxiing to the runway or just prior to landing, and after you have been told to "put your seats and trays in the upright position." In addition, whenever the captain is expecting turbulence and turns on the "Fasten Seat Belts" sign you should remain in your seat for your own safety. You are free to get up and use the washrooms at any other time.

A delayed flight is not only annoying, but also unnerving. What are the usual reasons for delays?

Delays in flights are never made lightly and only for very good reasons. You should remember that flight delays, while annoying, are always for the ultimate benefit of the passengers. You would not want the airline to fly a plane that was unsafe, just for the sake of maintaining a schedule, nor would you want to be left behind if your transferring flight was a few minutes late in landing. Crew members are aware of this, and to them a delay is re-assuring rather than unnerving.

If a flight has to be re-routed, this has to change the airline's whole schedule. How does this affect the crew? Are they expected to make their own way back to their base? What happens to the plane?

Certainly, whenever a flight is re-routed, changes to other flights and schedules have to be made to accommodate for the missing plane. Generally, the revised schedule will accommodate the re-routed plane and crew by slotting them, if possible, into another place in the schedule. Depending on where they are and the facilities available, the plane may be flown out and the crew sent home by another route. Sometimes they will stay with the plane and fly it out themselves.

Can electronic devices be used on a plane?

As a general rule, you can use most household types of equipment such as a tape recorder, a portable computer or a calculator during the flight except while taking off and landing. You will probably not be allowed to use a radio and certainly not a cellular telephone. The reason for this is that certain kinds of electronic equipment can interfere with the plane's radio and radar equipment. There is a list, available from the airline, of all electronic equipment that can or can not be used while in a plane.

If someone should panic on the plane, what is the very last point at which they could be let out?

Theoretically, a person could be let out at any time up to the actual take-off if the situation was serious enough. Certainly, if a person was upset enough, they could be let out at any time before the taxiing had started.

QUESTIONS ABOUT YOUR AIRCRAFT

It doesn't seem possible that a huge object like a jet airliner, with several hundred people inside it, can actually fly through the air. Just how does it fly, anyway?

The simplest answer to this question is that an aircraft flies because it is designed to fly. That is what it does. So long as it has propulsion to move it forward, allowing air to flow over and create a partial vacuum above the wings, the aircraft will lift off of the ground and fly. It is a flying machine; it has no other function but to fly. As long as everything is working properly, that is what it will do.

Looking into the cockpit on most airplanes, there seems to be hundreds of dials. How many are there, and what do they all mean?

There are certainly a lot of dials. There are at least ten for each engine alone. That makes forty right there. While it looks like a lot, remember there are two complete sets of controls in the cockpit - one for the pilot, and one for the co-pilot, so only half of the dials are being used at any one time. Any controls that require constant monitoring are also equipped with warning lights and signals which come on instantly if something is wrong. These work like the oil pressure and generator lights on your car. These instruments tell the pilots everything they need to know about their plane. The pilots are highly trained in their use and function, and while it seems a lot, they know what to watch for. On some of the newer planes, instrument panels have been replaced by computer screens or visual displays. These are known as "glass cockpits."

When does the pilot actually turn the engines on? Do they start one at a time, or all at once?

The aircraft's engines are started just prior to, or during, pushback, that is, when the plane is being pushed away from the terminal. They are started one at a time, so that the pilots can monitor each engine in turn as it "spools up."

What does "automatic pilot" mean, and when is it used?

The "automatic pilot" or "autopilot", is a term used to describe a number of different systems in a modern aircraft. These can actually perform the manual functions of the pilot. It is not unlike the cruise control on your car but of course it is vastly more complicated and performs a much wider function. Once the plane is airborne and on its proper course, the pilot enters heading, altitude, airspeed, etc., into a computer and engages the autopilot. The plane then flies itself using his programmed instructions. The pilot continues to monitor the controls constantly and can override the autopilot at any time for any reason. What the autopilot does is to relieve the pilot of most of the physical work of flying the plane, especially on the long stretches of the flight between take-off and landing. In actual fact, on the majority of flights, the autopilot is used most of the time the plane is in the air.

The autopilot can control the plane at any time after take-off and on descent to as low as eighty feet above the ground. Most pilots prefer to fly the plane manually at the lower altitudes. The autopilot actually does a better job of controlling the plane at higher altitudes because the thinner air makes it more difficult to maintain proper speed and altitude. While the autopilot can both take-off and land the plane if required, in practice this is seldom done. Virtually all take-offs and landings are performed manually by the pilot.

What are the flaps and what is their function?
What sound do flaps make?

The flaps are the long sections of the wing on the trailing (back) edge, which, when employed, will move out and downward from the wing. Their function is to lengthen and increase the curvature of the wing and by doing so, increase the lift of the plane. During landing, the flaps also create drag, which helps to slow the plane down. The flaps will be employed primarily during take off and landing, but you may also see them moving slightly in and out during flight, as the pilot steers the plane.

The sound of the flaps is quite noticeable. The heavy hydraulic motors used to move the flaps in and out make a high-pitched whining sound which lasts for a few seconds. Once the flaps are deployed, the drag created may also cause the plane to shudder quite noticeably.

What are the spoilers, and what do they do? What is the sound of the spoilers?

The spoilers are located on the top of the wing. They are the long flap-like sections that open upwards. When they are employed the air rushing over them makes a burbling sound.

Their purpose is to spoil or deflect the air flow over the wing so that the wing can no longer lift the airplane. They are employed during landing to push the weight of the plane down on to the runway and prevent it from lifting up again once it has touched down. They also aid in braking the plane. The spoilers are also used in the air during turning, (or banking, as it is called). They reduce lift on one of the wings, thus pushing it downward, allowing more lift on the other side. This causes the plane to turn in the direction of the lowered wing.

We are familiar with the noise of the flaps and the spoilers going up and down. What other noise changes may we experience during a flight?

There is a lot of equipment on a plane that makes a noise, and during a flight you may hear noises coming from a number of places. People seated near a washroom, for instance, are often startled by the sudden whoosh as someone flushes the toilet. Flight attendants operate equipment in their galleys, like garbage compactors or devices for moving storage compartments up and down, all of which may make sudden and unexpected noises.

There are two other sounds that you may want to listen for. First is the sound of the landing gear going up and down. During takeoff, just as the plane leaves the runway and starts to climb rapidly away from the airport, you will hear the sound of the landing gear being retracted. The landing gear are simply the wheels that sit underneath the plane when on the ground. During the flight the wheels are raised and stored inside the body of the plane. You will first hear the whining sound of the motors as they retract the heavy gear, followed by a fairly loud bump as the gear locks into its compartment and the doors close. Again, just as the pilot is getting ready to land, he will lower the landing gear. As it comes down it makes a loud clunk, followed by the rushing sound of the wind as the doors open, followed by another bump as the gear locks into landing position. Because the landing gear are very heavy, you will probably notice that the plane will shake and vibrate slightly when the wheels are down.

The other sound that often startles people is the sound of the engine thrust reversers. Just as the plane touches down on the runway, you will hear the engines change to a very loud, roaring sound. This is because the engines have been put into reverse thrust to help slow the aircraft. In fact you will actually feel the deceleration, like you would in a car when the brakes are applied hard. All that is happening is the air that was going through the engine is now being re-directed forward and sideways out of the back of the engine. On some planes you may also see what looks like a bucket extend down from the back of the engines. This is not something falling off the engine. It is simply a deflector, to channel the air forward and assist in slowing the plane down.

What is a stabilizer?

The stabilizers are located on the horizontal section of the tail. They make the aircraft climb or descend.

What are the ailerons?

The ailerons are located on the trailing (back) edge of the wings, and their function is to make the plane turn right or left. You will notice the ailerons moving very slightly almost all of the time during a flight as the pilot or the autopilot makes minor adjustments to the attitude of the plane.

What does the rudder do? Does it move?

The rudder is located in the tail of the plane and its function is to keep the plane going in a straight line. Jet planes make minimal use of the rudder. The great power of their engines are more effective in keeping the plane straight. A rudder is used more in propeller planes to counteract the torque effect of the propellers.

What is pressurization? How often does a plane become de-pressurized?

Pressurization is the means by which a breathable atmosphere is maintained inside the aircraft cabin. Above ten thousand feet, the outside air pressure is not sufficient to provide human beings with enough oxygen to breathe properly. They would soon lose consciousness at the higher altitudes that aircraft normally fly. The pressurization system pumps up the air inside the plane to a simulated altitude of under ten thousand feet allowing the passengers and crew to breathe normally without the use of oxygen masks.

De-pressurization can occur, either by a failure in the pressurization system, or by a rupture in the skin of the plane. This is a very rare occurrence indeed, but should it happen then two things would take place. First, the oxygen masks located near each seat would drop down automatically. (They are held up by the pressure inside the plane - if it drops, then they fall down by themselves.) Passengers could then breathe the oxygen coming through the masks. Secondly, the pilot would immediately bring the plane down to an altitude below ten thousand feet, where the pressure is higher and can provide enough natural oxygen for the people on board. He would then, undoubtedly land at the nearest suitable airport and have the system repaired before continuing on to the destination.

What happens if the air intake system fails?

There will always be more than one ventilation system on your plane. If one should fail, the others will carry on to ensure that air is getting in. In a complete shut-down, de-pressurization would occur, the oxygen masks would come down, and the pilot would descend the plane to a lower altitude.

Who determines how much fuel should be taken on for each flight?

Fuel requirements are carefully calculated for each flight according to the type of plane, the distance to be travelled, the prevailing winds and weather, the route to be flown, the weight to be carried and many other factors. Before each flight the pilot is provided with these calculations and he then has the final say on how much fuel he is to carry. The fuel carried on any flight is based on the minimum required for that flight taking into account all the various factors that may affect it. Indeed, it is against the law to carry less than the minimum amount required. As well as the basic fuel requirements your plane is also required to carry enough fuel to enable it to get to a specified alternate airport should it be unable to land at its original destination and enough fuel to enable it to circle the alternate airport in the event of a traffic backup.

Is all fuel stored in the wings?

Most fuel is stored in the wings, although some aircraft also carry fuel in auxiliary tanks located in the fuselage between the wings. Still others are designed to hold fuel in the horizontal stabilizer located in the tail. This is simply a matter of design.

What kind of fuel goes into a jet?

Commercial jet aircraft use a kerosene-based fuel known as Jet-A1. Jet fuel is evolving continuously and the fuel includes various additives like flame retardant chemicals as added safety measures.

Does the crew make a list of faults that they may experience with the plane during a flight, for correction once they land? What happens to that list?

Aircraft are very complicated, sophisticated machines, and, like any other machine, things can and do go wrong with them. Any problem, from a burned out light bulb to a major engine malfunction is recorded in a log book with numbered pages and several copies. There are very strict company and government regulations setting out how these malfunctions must be corrected. Minor malfunctions, like light bulbs, or trouble with a coffee-maker, for instance, must be repaired within ten days. Major ones, like engine or control problems, must be corrected immediately. During flight, the pilots will record any malfunctions noted, and this record is handed in at the end of the flight. If any major problem recorded has not been corrected, the pilot may refuse to fly the plane. These log books become permanent records and are audited regularly by the airline maintenance staff and government regulators.

You often see the pilot or another officer walking around the plane prior to take-off. What are they doing?

Yes, they are really looking for something. They are checking for any possible damage to the aircraft, like cuts in the tires, breaks in the skin, or any other obvious mechanical defects. Some airlines have maintenance people do this check rather than the pilots. It's just one more check to ensure that the plane is in top flying condition.

Are there back-up systems on a plane in case something should fail?

A back-up system operates in conjunction with the main system. It will take over and do the job should the main system fail for any reason. Suffice it to say that there are numerous back-up systems covering every major component of an aircraft. Every aircraft type is different and every aircraft system is different, but in general, any part of the plane that is involved in flight control, passenger safety, or communication is covered by at least one back-up system. The more crucial the system, the more back-ups there are to take over in case of a failure.

Is it true that the wings on the plane move a few feet during flight? How much movement is there? Can they break off? What would happen if one did?

They certainly do move. If they didn't flex, then the pressures that these huge structures endure would most certainly cause them to break. On the very large planes, like a 747, for example, the movement in the wing can be anything up to nine or ten feet up or down. Very simply, this flexibility is designed to prevent the wings from snapping off. An aircraft's wings, while protruding from each side of the fuselage, are not two separate structures. They are, in fact, one huge beam supporting the fuselage in the middle. Breakage of this structure is so rare as to be virtually impossible during normal flight conditions, which include the very worst turbulence or weather conditions that you can imagine.

How much stress can a plane take?

Stress in aircraft is measured in G's. One G equals the force of gravity. Aircraft attachment points are designed to sustain nine G's forward load, two G's sideload, and four to five G's of vertical load. That's an awful lot of stress. Aircraft are typically over-designed. That is not to say that a heavy commercial aircraft would withstand the kind of stress during sustained aerobatics that a military fighter would. Any amount of turbulence, or even a severe emergency situation, would be easily handled by a commercial airliner's airframe.

Is it true that a plane is built in segments to give it flexibility?

Aircraft are built in segments, mainly for ease of manufacturing. The various segments are designed to take loads in many different ways and it is true that they will flex during flight. Just like the wings, it is this flexibility, rather than rigidity, of the design that gives the plane its strength.

What is metal fatigue?

Any time metal is bent, it is weakened. Bend any piece of metal back and forth enough times and it will break. Try doing it to a paper clip. That is metal fatigue. Metal fatigue in an aircraft can occur when the stresses encountered during flight cause the metal components to stretch and contract constantly. In time, as with any other metal object, this constant back and forth motion can cause the component to break. Aircraft are inspected regularly for signs of metal fatigue, particularly in the major components of the planes. When found it is repaired immediately.

What is the vibration that I feel when I step onto the plane? It seems that the coffee is perking, cabin lights are on, and the music is playing, yet the engine isn't turned on yet. Where does the power come from?

While on the ground, the aircraft is supplied with electrical power either from a ground power unit, which is plugged into the aircraft, or from a generator mounted on the aircraft itself. The vibration is probably coming from the air conditioning systems or the auxiliary power unit. Once the plane is moving under its own power the electricity is supplied by its own internal generators.

What is that big black pipe that leads from the terminal to the plane when it is docked?

The black duct supplies pre-conditioned air into the cabin from an outside air conditioning unit. This is simply a way of providing air to the plane without having to use the aircraft's internal system.

Why is the air so dry on the plane?

The ventilation system on your plane draws in fresh air from the outside and expels the stale air. Air in the upper atmosphere has almost no moisture, which is why the air being drawn in feels so dry. The air inside the plane is exchanged, that is, replaced by fresh air from outside approximately every two to two and a half minutes depending on the type of aircraft.

Is it true that the luggage is carefully stowed so that the weight is distributed evenly? Why is this done?

The weight carried by an aircraft must be evenly distributed throughout the plane to make it easier and safer to fly. Before the luggage and freight is loaded, each cart is weighed in the terminal and a computer assigns the cart to a specific area of the plane.

Is it true that passengers are seated so as to distribute weight evenly? How can you tell if they're light or heavy?

Like the luggage, the weight of the passengers should be distributed as evenly as possible throughout the cabin. To do this, rather than weigh each passenger, a standard weight, such as 200 lbs for a male, 150 lbs for a female is used to estimate the total weight of the passengers. The computer will then assign passengers to certain areas of the plane in order to achieve a proper weight distribution. Passengers are unaware of this of course, but seating is very carefully assigned in order to maintain proper distribution of weight. Occasionally, when a large number of large people, like a football team for instance, are travelling together, other passengers will be reassigned to compensate for the extra weight in one area of the plane. Weight distribution is less crucial once the plane is in the air. People moving around or changing seats once the plane is airborne can be compensated for by the flight controls, but for take-off and landing, the flight attendants will make sure that everyone is in their proper seat.

How heavy is a jet airliner?

Incredible as it may seem, they are very heavy objects indeed. The weight of an airliner can be anywhere from five hundred to five thousand tons.

How much does a plane cost?

The cost of a plane obviously depends on its size, capacity, and age. A modern commercial aircraft today can cost upwards of one hundred million dollars. In addition to the plane, an airline must also keep a huge inventory of spare parts and replacement equipment in order to keep the plane airworthy. A certain stock of all these spare parts has to be kept at all the terminals used on a regular basis by that airline. Flying a plane is a very expensive business.

Just how fast can a plane go? How fast does it go during take-off? During flight?

Virtually all commercial airliners are designed for sub-sonic flight, meaning below the speed of sound, which is approximately 700 miles per hour, depending on the plane's altitude and other factors. Supersonic flight, that is, above the speed of sound, requires a completely different aircraft design. At present the Concorde is the only commercial airliner that is capable of supersonic flight. Take-off speed depends on the type of aircraft and many other things such as the density of the outside air, but it is probably around one hundred and fifty knots, which is equal to one hundred and seventy-two miles per hour. To cover the distance from any two points on the ground, most commercial airliners will travel around 500 to 550 mph. Airspeed, that is, the speed that the plane is actually travelling through the air, is measured not in miles per hour, but in relation to the speed of sound. Since this varies according to the altitude and other factors, it is difficult to equate air speed with miles per hour. Airspeed is usually quoted as a Mach number, with the number equalling the relation of the speed of the plane to the speed of sound at that altitude. Mach 0.75, for example, would mean the plane is travelling at 75% of the speed of sound at that altitude.

What type of emergency equipment do you carry on board the plane?

Every aircraft carries a number of special fire extinguishers, oxygen equipment and first aid kits. There would also be fire axes, a full-face mask and fire mitts which would allow crew members to actively combat fire and smoke. In addition, each plane carries an extensive doctors' kit. This would contain catheters, injectable medication, blood pressure cuffs and everything a doctor might need to make a diagnosis and begin emergency treatment of a sick or injured passenger. This kit would be made available to a physician who happened to be on board.

As we get on the plane, we can see the pilots studying something in the cockpit. What exactly are they studying?

Before taking off, all the flight-deck crew are involved in a detailed and comprehensive check of all the important systems on that aircraft. These include a check of fuel levels, all the electrical and hydraulic systems, radio and radar equipment. This check continues right up until the time that the plane actually leaves the runway. While the plane is taxiing toward the runway, the pilots are checking the operations of the engines, the brakes, the weight and balance of the plane and the flight controls. As the engines are being powered up just prior to starting the take-off run, the pilots check the engines for perfect operation. Any malfunction and the take-off would be aborted immediately.

Another important procedure, prior to take-off, is a review of the emergency procedures, both as a team and individually, to be sure that each member of the crew is fully aware of their function and duties in the event of an emergency.

Passengers are required to fasten their seatbelts well before take-offs and landings, but the flight attendants buckle up only seconds before the plane starts down the runway. Also, flight attendants seem to have more secure seatbelts than the passengers.

Not only are flight attendants required by law to buckle

up during take off and landings, just like the passengers, but you will notice that the safety belts they use are of a different, stronger and more comprehensive design as well. To put it bluntly, this is to ensure that, should there be an accident at this time, the flight attendants will survive and be able to supervise an evacuation and assist passengers.

The flight attendants are responsible for the safety of their passengers both before take-off and during and after landing. They are busy checking on the safety of the passengers right up to the last minute before the plane leaves the ground. Survivability of the passengers depends absolutely on the cabin crew and it is important that they be ready to assist the passengers immediately following an accident.

Is it true that if the landing gear will not come down for landing, the crew can bring it down manually?

In the event that the landing gear should fail to come down by the normal procedure, all aircraft have a number of backup procedures, which would include actually winding down the gear by hand. But even if all those backup procedures should fail, it is still a very heavy piece of equipment and simply opening the doors and releasing the locking mechanism will cause the gear to come down by the force of gravity and air pressure.

What would happen if one engine failed, or if all engines failed?

The failure of one engine, or even more than one engine, on a multi-engine aircraft is not that serious a problem. All aircraft with more than one engine must, by law, be capable of flying and landing, with a full load, using only one of its engines. Nevertheless, should an engine fail while in flight, as a safety precaution the pilot would most probably either turn around and return to the airport from where you took off or decide to land at the nearest suitable airport. There, either the engine would be repaired, or the passengers switched to another aircraft. The most serious effect on the passengers would probably be a delay in their journey.

Should all engines fail at the same time, obviously the matter is rather more serious. But even without engine power, a modern aircraft is still capable of gliding for a considerable distance. In fact, a streamlined, modern jet aircraft can glide thirty miles for every ten thousand feet of altitude. On major air traffic routes an aircraft is never out of contact with the ground and would almost certainly be able to reach an airport somewhere along its route. Your plane has auxiliary power units operated by wind power, that would continue to provide electricity to the essential equipment such as the flight controls and radios. It is highly likely that the pilot would be able to glide down and make a fairly normal landing. The loss of power would make the plane more difficult to control, but even in a normal, powered landing, the engines are throttled right back to idle just before touching down and the loss of power on the descent would not make a lot of difference to the actual landing. Pilots are trained in this procedure and practice doing engine failure landings as part of their ongoing training.

What would happen if an engine caught fire during a flight?

All the engines are equipped with fire extinguishing mechanisms that can be activated by the pilots from the cockpit. In the event of a fire in one of the engines, the pilots would first shut the engine down and cut off all fuel, hydraulic fluid and power to that engine. If the fire still persisted, a fire extinguishing agent would be released into the engine, followed by a second fire extinguishing agent thirty seconds later, if necessary. The loss of one engine would not be a serious problem, but the pilot would probably decide to land at the nearest airport.

We sometimes hear of a tire blowing out during a take off or landing. What happens if a tire blows?

A blown tire during take-off or landing is not serious. Often, this can happen without the crew being aware of it. A large airplane has a number of wheels, sometimes as many as eighteen or twenty, and the loss of one, or even more than one, does not affect the landing or take-off very much. Once a blown tire is discovered it is replaced immediately.

How come we hear of baggage doors being left unlocked?

While this has happened, it is nevertheless an extremely unusual situation. All doors on the plane are physically checked from the outside before the plane moves off the ramp. In addition, the plane has an alarm system which informs the pilot immediately if any door is unlocked. He will not move the plane until any alarm is checked out.

When and under what circumstances will a plane dump fuel? Does this pollute the environment?

Very occasionally, an aircraft may have to dump excess fuel by releasing it into the air There are a number of reasons why a plane may have to do this, most connected to the weight of the plane. When fuel dumping is required there are prescribed zones, usually located over water, for this purpose. Undoubtedly, the release of aviation fuel into the atmosphere does add to pollution, which is why it is done so infrequently and only when there is no alternative. Another factor is the very high cost of fuel. Airlines are understandably reluctant to simply dump valuable fuel unnecessarily. There is no risk to the airplane when fuel is dumped. The fuel is very thin and vaporizes immediately as it hits the atmosphere where it is swept away by the slipstream.

What speed is needed before a plane can take off?

This varies with the weight and type of the plane. As you might expect, the heavier the plane, the more speed is required to lift it off of the ground. As a general rule a plane will be travelling between 140 and 200 miles per hour on the runway at the time of lift-off.

Why does the pilot sometimes have to make those steep turns after take-off, and prior to landing? It feels like we are tipping over. Will we?

Just as you might make a sharp turn into your own driveway, sometimes a pilot has to steer sharply in one direction or another to turn his plane onto the proper approach to the airport. Similarly, following take-off he sometimes has to turn sharply onto the flight path designated for him to clear the vicinity of the airport. No, the plane won't tip over and no, the passengers won't fall out. Pilots don't like having to make these sharp turns, because they are disconcerting for their passengers. Mostly they are required by noise abatement regulations or because of other traffic in the area.

Sometimes during takeoff, the plane will climb sharply. Then the noise will change and one feels a dropping sensation before the plane climbs again. It is as if the take-off is done in stages. Is this what is happening?

Yes, basically that is what is happening. When this happens the pilot will climb steeply to get away from the ground, possibly due to noise abatement regulations, or to avoid buildings or other obstacles around the airport. After clearing the airport, he will level off for a while causing the dropping sensation, (you're not really dropping, simply not climbing any more.) Then, after a while, he will climb again to reach his assigned altitude. Sometimes, the pilot must perform fairly extensive maneouvering during takeoff to avoid obstacles or other planes in the area.

We sometimes read about near-misses. How many such near-misses would a pilot experience, on average?

Despite what we may hear in the news the number of near-misses, when two planes come near to colliding, is very small indeed in relation to the number of planes in the air at any one time. Often, such reports are based on subjective sightings by a passenger, who is not aware that while two planes may be near to each other, both pilots are in complete control and in no danger of colliding. Newer planes are equipped with a Traffic Collision Avoidance System, (T.C.A.S.), which gives the pilots instant warning of another plane in their airspace.

How does a pilot know that he is lined up with the runway for landing?

When an aircraft begins its final approach it is probably still several miles from the end of the runway, yet it invariably touches down in just the right spot. If the approach is through cloud or fog this feat seems even more amazing. The pilot is guided to the exact spot for touchdown by a number of signals. Most importantly, a radio beam from the ground to the plane tells him exactly when he is on the right heading. In addition, once he can see the runway he is also guided by runway lights and other visual signals. Finally, if all else fails, the computer system on board the aircraft is quite capable of landing the plane without assistance from the pilots. Of course, the pilots would closely monitor the landing during such an occurrence.

Just after touch-down there is often a loud roaring sound. What is going on?

Nothing to worry about. As soon as the plane has touched the ground, the pilot must immediately start to slow it down so that he doesn't run right off the end of the runway. To do that he will often use the terrific power of the engines as a brake. He will activate deflectors which direct the thrust of the engines forward instead of backward and actually push against the plane slowing it down. That roaring sound you hear is the sound of the thrust from the engines pushing against the deflectors and onto the ground.

Sometimes during landing, the pilot seems to rock the plane from side to side. Why is this?

The pilot will sometimes have to do this in order to manoeuvre the plane through cross winds. The pilot is compensating for the varying amounts of side-to-side movement that gusts of wind are subjecting the aircraft to. The design of some planes make this rocking necessary in order to descend more evenly under windy conditions.

Sometimes the plane will appear to bounce when it touches down. Does it bounce?

A plane can bounce, that is, leave the ground momentarily after touch-down, but not usually. That bouncing feeling is more likely the sensation of the plane settling down onto its landing gear, which acts like a giant shock-absorber.

Each landing seems to be different - why is that?

No two landings are exactly the same. Some may be feather-light with almost no sensation of touching the ground, while others may make contact with a frightening thump. Sometimes the pilot seems to be inching gingerly toward the ground, while another time the plane seems to descend with no hesitation at all. Each landing is different and the reason for the difference depends on a number of factors. Weather, winds, the weight of the plane, the temperature, all affect the way in which the plane will be landed. Another factor may be nothing more than a particular pilot's personal style.

How close to the airport does the pilot turn on the big landing lights? Do they only go on at night? How far does the beam extend?

The landing lights will normally go on about thirty miles away from the aiport. They are used both in daylight and in darkness. The beam will probably extend for about a mile.

Is the beam of the landing lights reduced in fog or snow?

A plane can land quite safely without the landing lights. Just as a car's headlights in fog or snow will reflect back to the driver, so the landing lights will sometimes get in the way of the pilot and he will turn them off.

What are those blue lights on the runway for? Are they always blue, or does each terminal have a different colour?

Runway lights are standard for all airports throughout the world. Blue lights indicate taxi-ways, that is, the path an airplane follows to the terminal once it has turned off the runway. White lights indicate a runway. The end of the runway is marked by red lights and the corners with amber lights.

Does the black box, or the flight recorder, record all conversations in the cockpit?

All communication within the cockpit, including radio traffic and conversations between the crew members, is recorded by the flight recorder. It can not be turned off for any reason, by anyone in the plane.

How serious a problem would make the pilot decide to: abort a take-off, abort a landing, turn back to the airport, delay a flight or make an emergency landing?

Once the pilot has received the necessary clearance and started his take-off run, only a very serious problem like an engine or a flight control malfunction would cause him to abort the take-off. Once the plane has reached a speed of 100 knots or so, aborting take-off would be very serious as he would probably not be able to stop the plane before it reached the end of the runway. More likely, he would take off as usual and then immediately circle and land again. Pilots are trained to handle just this situation and they practice it constantly.

To abort a landing may simply be a case of not being completely satisfied with the approach and deciding to go around and try again. Alternatively, ground control may have requested a go around because of delays on the ground. The pilot may have a malfunction warning and may want some time to try to locate and correct the problem before landing. One thing is certain. The plane must be landed eventually and it is better that the pilot land the plane rather than waste time and fuel and create stress by delaying. Again, pilots are rigidly trained in all kinds of aborted landing procedures and practice them constantly.

A pilot may decide to turn back to the airport for any number of reasons, not all of them serious. There may be a minor malfunction to be repaired and there are no facilities available at his destination. There may be a problem with one of the passengers, sudden illness, for example.

Returning to the airport may be better than carrying on for several hours before assistance can be obtained and the pilot has to weigh all these factors before deciding to turn back.

If a flight is delayed, it is usually due to a problem somewhere along the route - weather, a strike at the destination, or scheduling difficulties. Anybody who travels frequently is familiar with this situation.

An emergency landing is, of course, a much more serious problem, and would only be done in the case of a severe in-flight emergency. Emergency landings are very rare indeed, and while pilots and flight attendants are trained and practice the procedures constantly, most commercial pilots have never actually performed an emergency landing. Should it become necessary to perform such a landing, the flight crew and the airport will immediately put in place emergency landing procedures for the protection of the passengers and to prepare them for the very worst things that could happen. In fact, in those rare cases when emergency landings have been performed, the plane seldom actually crashes, because proven procedures have been put in place to prepare the pilot, crew and passengers for that eventuality.

Is it true that planes flying in an easterly direction fly the odd numbers and westerly planes fly even numbers?

Just like the centre line on a highway, aircraft are separated from each other, but by altitude. Up to 29,000 feet, all westbound flights fly at even number whole altitudes, 22,000 feet, 24,000 feet, 26,000 feet and so on. All eastbound flights fly at odd number whole altitudes, 21,000 feet, 23,000 feet, 25,000 feet. This maintains at least 1,000 feet separation between flights approaching each other in opposite directions. Above 29,000 feet, where the air is thinner and exact altitudes are a little more difficult to maintain, planes fly in 2,000 feet separations, 31,000 feet westbound, 33,000 feet eastbound and so on.

Does the plane stay at the same altitude and in the same corridor all through the flight? What would happen if the pilot switched corridors?

It's not really a big thing to change altitudes or corridors during a flight. The pilot can decide to change altitudes or corridors at any time for any good reason, such as avoiding turbulence. As the plane uses up its fuel supply it gets lighter, and because of the change in weight, it has a natural ability to fly higher. A pilot will often take advantage of this opportunity to fly a little higher where fuel consumption is less than at lower altitudes. The chance of turbulence is lessened as well.

How does a pilot know what's up ahead when flying through clouds or darkness? Could there be another plane, or a mountain?

Pilots can see just as well in clouds, thick fog, or darkness as they can in broad daylight. The radar on board the plane identifies any weather in their vicinity. If there was another plane anywhere in the vicinity of yours, it would appear on the air traffic controller's screen on the ground, as well as on the T.C.A.S. system on board the plane. Remember that the ground controllers are aware of where your plane is in relation to any other traffic in the area, regardless of whether or not your pilot can see through the clouds or the dark sky.

Mountains are not likely to get in the way because the cruising altitude of any large airplane is well above the height of even the highest mountains. Throughout your flight, your pilots are constantly keeping track of their position, both vertically and horizontally and the ground controllers are doing the same.

If everybody on board a plane suddenly decided to get up and look out of the right-hand windows at the same time, would

the shift in weight make the plane tip to that side?

The shift in weight would be noticed by the pilots but they would compensate immediately by a simple adjustment in their controls.

QUESTIONS ABOUT AIR TRAFFIC CONTROL

There are many air traffic controllers in the tower at the same time, watching a lot of planes. How does our air traffic controller know what the other controllers in the tower are doing? If they all have planes to watch how do they communicate with each other?

The operations in the control tower are very carefully integrated. Each controller does his job, his whole job and nothing more than his job. Therefore, when a plane is handed over to another controller, that controller knows that all necessary conditions have been complied with.

Before a flight, at what point does contact with the plane start?

While still at the boarding gate, all pilots are required to call a position in the tower called clearance delivery. They usually start communicating with the tower about ten minutes or so before the aircraft doors are closed. They inform the controller who they are and where they are going and must receive authority, under specified flight conditions in order to proceed.

What message is given at the end of the runway for take-off? How much time is given to the pilot to complete the procedure?

Once the controllers are sure that the departure end of the runway is clear, they inform the pilot that he is cleared for takeoff. They also provide him with wind direction and speed, and the radio frequency to be used. Once takeoff clearance has been issued and acknowledged by the pilot, he must take off immediately. Normally, pilots will not enter a runway unless they are completely ready to take off.

How much of a time lapse is there between planes taking off?

All that is really required between take-offs is just enough time to be sure that planes will miss each other. In other words, about a micro-second! However, in practice, planes using the same runway, of the same weight and speed and going in the same direction, should be allowed a minimum of approximately 45 seconds between take-off clearances. This equates to about three nautical miles between planes once they are in the air. Take-off clearances from the air traffic controllers are rarely done that tightly, although this will depend on the volume of traffic at any individual airport. If there is a slow plane ahead of a fast one, or a large commercial jet ahead of a small, lighter private plane, the smaller one may wait up to six minutes in some circumstances.

One of the important factors in take-off times is the possibility and magnitude of wing-tip vortices, also known as wake turbulence. These are swirling pockets of air created by the wings of a large plane which create dangerous turbulence for the plane following behind. The thing to remember is that take-offs are closely watched by the air traffic controllers, who have an over-view of the whole control area and will allow a plane to take-off only when it is absolutely safe to do so.

Does the time lapse between planes taking off vary from airport to airport?

Yes it does. The time allowed between take-offs at a high altitude airport, such as Calgary or Denver, for example, is a little longer than would be allowed at a sea-level airport like Vancouver or New York. This is because the ability of a plane to lift is dependent on the density of the air. The combination of high altitude and high temperature together would require even more time. Lift factors for all the different types of planes are carefully calculated for each individual airport and the time between take-offs are adjusted accordingly.

How do air traffic controllers sort out the light planes from the big commercial ones? Who looks after the private aircraft?

An airplane is an airplane and all are treated the same, depending on the rules under which they operate. These rules differ according to the type of equipment, its maximum altitude and other factors. Separating the smaller planes from the large ones involves getting the heavy aircraft off the runway and on their way as quickly as possible, allowing smaller planes to operate at lower altitudes than the large ones. This is usually controlled by visual means directly from the control tower. Each airport will stipulate a certain minimum level of equipment, such as radio equipment, size of the planes, etc. that will be permitted to use their facilities.

Do air traffic controllers talk with the pilots until they are out of their zone? How far is that?

Yes they do. The range varies from airport to airport but, generally speaking, the air traffic controllers at the airport of departure remain in contact for about forty miles, at which time the plane is handed off to the next facility.

What is the radius of the air traffic control's radar to planes?

This varies from area to area. In the Calgary, Alberta area, for example, the radar has a range of 220 nautical miles. Other airports have different ranges, depending on their location and proximity to other airports.

Does the pilot communicate only with air traffic control, or does he speak to other people as well?

Throughout the flight, the aircraft is in contact with any number of people on the ground. Airlines are required to maintain their own communication networks, which are used to pass along information about loads, connecting flights and other information concerning the company. Sometimes this network will be very basic, but in the case of the major airlines they can be very sophisticated, even to the extent of monitoring the performance of the plane while in flight. Pilots are in almost constant communication with somebody during a flight, such as air traffic control, their own communications network, even pilots of other planes flying nearby.

Is there any time on a flight when the pilot cannot contact an air traffic controller?

Every commercial aircraft is in constant touch with a ground controller, the whole time the plane is in the air. The range for any ground station is about 200 miles and after that contact is passed to another station within range of the aircraft. The air traffic control network covers virtually the entire world and the chances of a plane being completely out of contact within that network are so slight as to be non-existent.

When a plane is passing over land, it is in constant contact by radar. Over water, contact is by way of high frequency radio and control is by way of position reports provided by each pilot. As the plane reaches certain specified positions, identified by degrees of longitude and latitude, the pilot reports to the controller. In this way, the exact position of each and every plane in an oceanic area is known and plotted on a huge plotting board.

Modern aircraft systems are so reliable and have so many back-up systems, that complete radio failure is extremely unlikely. Even in the unlikely event of a total failure, air traffic control can still operate without the use of radio or radar.

If there are two planes using the same corridor, how close behind one another should they be?

The distance between two planes in the same corridor is governed, to some extent, by their speed. A fast plane following a slow one, for example, will change altitude in order to go by. Generally speaking, two planes at the same approximate speed must maintain a distance of three to five miles between them.

At what range can the control tower pick up an incoming plane?

Generally speaking, contact with planes starts when they enter about a forty nautical mile radius from the airport. It is important to know that virtually everywhere in the world where planes fly, an aircraft is under somebody's control from the ground. Planes are controlled by reports received from pilots reporting their altitude, destination, direction and other important information through a worldwide high-frequency radio network operated under the auspices of the International Civil Aviation Organization. The links in this network are spread across the continent, and form part of the North Atlantic network. In the North Pacific, links are Vancouver, Alaska, Tokyo, San Francisco and Guam. The entire world is covered by such radio networks and an aircraft is always in contact all along its route.

At what point does air traffic control prepare the crew for descent? What is the procedure?

Normally, the pilot initiates the request for permission to descend, once he is near his destination. Under some conditions, however, a pilot may be requested to descend by air traffic control, due to traffic conditions, weather, or other factors.

How do the air traffic controllers help a plane to prepare for landing?

The pilot has the ultimate responsibility for his aircraft. Air traffic control is there to ensure safe and expeditious movement of the aircraft only. In other words, air traffic control makes the way clear for the pilot to land. They also provide information, such as the weather, the required altimeter setting and runway surface conditions on which the pilot makes the decision whether or not to land.

During descent, what do the pilot and the control tower talk about?

Generally, they exchange information such as the plane's altitude, speed and the choice of runway.

Does the pilot ever miss the runway when trying to land? What happens in this case?

While this doesn't happen very often, it does happen occasionally, usually in bad weather conditions like fog or rain. Should this happen, the pilot would commence a go-around procedure. This involves lifting the plane again, making a wide circle away from the airport and re-positioning the plane for another attempt. Pilots practice this procedure constantly and there are rules laid down for its use.

How do air traffic control decide which runway will be used?

As a general rule, aircraft take off and land into the wind. Air traffic control are monitoring wind speed and direction constantly and specify the runway that provides the best conditions for landing or taking off.

What is a holding pattern?

Very often, there are more planes trying to land at a busy airport than the ground facilities or the ground controllers can deal with all at once. Like traffic on a highway, planes waiting to land sometimes have to line-up for a while until the ground can deal with them. This line-up in the sky is called a holding pattern. It is simply a path in the sky in which planes waiting to land at an airport fly until they can be dealt with in an orderly and safe manner. Aircraft entering the holding pattern over an airport are given an exact location and height at which to cruise to await landing instructions from the ground. The planes are stacked in a spiral pattern, separated from each other in layers of one thousand feet in altitude. As the first plane in the stack lands, all those above it descend to the next level and any new planes join the stack at the top. The holding pattern is utilized until all the planes in the stack are landed safely.

Are all control tower rules international rules?

The rules governing control towers and air traffic control in general are very much the same all over the world. There are minor differences from country to country, of course, but the intent and content of the regulations are almost identical.

If the airport closes, is the control tower manned anyway?

Normally, the control tower is manned even if the airport is closed. While they may not wish, or be able to, land, there may still be planes in the airspace to be looked after.

Why is the control tower always set away from the terminal?

While it is important that the control tower be near the airport terminal, it is usually set some distance away, mainly for reasons of security. In fact, in many airports, the control towers are not even on the airport property at all.

The tower has big windows, from which the air traffic controllers can see all over the airport. Do they go more by their radar screens or what they can actually see?

They use both radar and visual information. The large, fast, heavy planes are first lined up onto the runway using radar when they are still many miles away. On their approach to the airport they are controlled from the radar screens, until the time that the controllers in the tower can actually see them and guide them on to the ground.

Is the tower manned 24 hours a day, 365 days a year?

Certainly in all major airports, the control tower is manned around the clock, every day. This is not always the case in smaller airports but this does not mean that they cannot be used, nor would it prevent a plane from landing. If a plane must land at a smaller, unmanned airport, the pilot has procedures available to allow him to do this. In some smaller, unmanned airports the pilot of an incoming plane can turn on the runway lights by radio signal from the cockpit.

Who talks to the control tower from the plane - the pilot or first officer?

That depends on who is actually flying the plane at that time. During a flight, the flying duties, that is the actual flying of the plane, are shared between the captain and the first officer. At any time, one of these officers will be the flying pilot and the other the non-flying pilot. Communication between the plane and the ground is handled by whichever pilot is non-flying at any particular time.

Who has the final say on traffic flow, air traffic control or the pilots?

Only air traffic control has all the information concerning planes in the area, destinations, flight conditions, etc. and, quite logically, they have the final say on the movement of planes within their air space. Nevertheless, a pilot on board a plane also has very good reason for wanting to know what is happening as there could be circumstances in which he would want to move contrary to the controller's instructions. Normally, pilots will defer to the controllers, but should a dispute arise, the pilot does have the final say.

Do airports have a curfew, or a quiet time, to avoid noise pollution?

Many airports do, particularly those located near major

cities. Noise abatement is accomplished in various ways. Some airports use a system of preferential runways. These are runways where the flight path does not cross residential areas. Others might assign each airline a quota of permissible noise. When their noise quota is used up for a certain period, airport facilities may be restricted until the next period.

Noise pollution around airports is a major concern for city officials, residents and airport managers. Airlines try to do whatever is necessary to reduce noise wherever possible. However, they are also aware of the need for safety and noise control has to be secondary to safety considerations.

What about rules for noise pollution, are they the same at each terminal?

There are no common rules governing noise and noise pollution around airports, but those that are in place do tend to be similar. Each area responds to the problem in its own way. Frankfurt, Germany and London, England, have very strict requirements governing noise. In the United States, where some airports are privately owned, the problem of noise is sometimes controlled by a system of allotting each airline using the airport a certain number of decibels per day. These can be spread over one noisy plane or several quieter ones.

In the United States and Canada, the government has control over commercial aviation. How strict are they, with regard to adherence to rules, regulations and safety checks? Are all governments the same?

The governments of each country set rules governing aviation within their own country and generally, these rules are very strict. Airlines are checked constantly. Inspectors arrive unannounced for flights. Infractions can result in a license to operate being suspended or lifted. As well, they control the qualifications for people working in the industry, all documentation and procedures. In fact, there are very few aspects of commercial aviation that are not overseen by federal regulation. Generally speaking, governments in all countries make and enforce aviation rules. In addition, most countries subscribe to an international convention which sets rules for international aviation.

Is English the international language of aviation?

While English is usually spoken by pilots and air traffic controllers around the world, it is not really the official language of aviation. The official language consists of a lexicon or an international language of common words and phrases used and understood by anyone who flies internationally. The lexicon is based on English. Listening to a controller in Moscow, talking to a pilot from Great Britain, the language would sound very much like English, but would actually be made up of words and phrases which may be understood by the controller only in the context of the flight situation. The Canadian Government also publishes a French language lexicon for use in Canadian airports.

QUESTIONS ABOUT THE WEATHER

What happens if the plane is struck by lightning?

Occasionally, a lightning flash will strike a plane. These aircraft are designed to withstand a lightning strike without any danger to the plane or the passengers. The lightning simply passes through the plane and is led away by special defusers located on the trailing edges of the wings and stabilizers. The pilots have special lights in the cockpit which helps them reduce the flash. Pilots avoid flying through storms whenever possible. The danger is not the lightning but the turbulence associated with storms.

Who orders de-icing? How soon prior to take-off should this procedure be carried out? How long does the de-icing coating last?

De-icing is a procedure in which special chemicals are sprayed on the wings of a plane to prevent the build up of ice while grounded. Ice forming on the wings will change the airflow over the wing and affect the way the plane handles. This de-icing procedure can be ordered by the ground maintenance crew or the captain of the plane, with each one having the power to over-rule the other in favour of safety. Should the captain feel that de-icing is necessary and maintenance, for whatever reason, does not, then de-icing would be done. De-icing is done as close to take-off as possible to prevent the solution from simply running off the wing. The de-icing coating lasts only through the take-off procedure. Once the plane is air-borne, it will use its own internal de-icing system to take care of any ice that may form in the air.

What is the solution used for de-icing?

There are a number of solutions used for de-icing, depending on the severity of the weather, the temperature and the location. Most contain glycol, the main ingredient in automotive anti-freeze.

Is de-icing mandatory at certain temperatures, or in all cold climates?

De-icing is mandatory whenever there is ice present on the wing. This is the case in cold as well as temperate climates. The decision to spray the wings is the responsibility of the captain and the ground maintenance people.

What can cause a sudden drop in altitude? Does this occur often? Where is it most likely to occur?

A sudden drop in altitude, sometimes erroneously referred to as an air pocket, happens when a plane is riding a wave of air, which takes a sudden drop. This is most likely to occur when travelling over mountains. The air in which the plane is riding follows the contour of the mountaintops, and when it passes over a particularly high point, the plane rides down the slope just as if it were on the ground. It is simply a form of turbulence. All planes in the vicinity experience the same phenomenon, meaning that there will be no loss of separation.

What is turbulence?

Turbulence is simply erratic or bumpy flight conditions, which can be caused by many things, some of more concern than others. The simplest, and probably the most common type, is called mechanical turbulence. This is caused by the wind blowing over large objects on the ground, like mountains or a large city. This causes bumps and hollows in the air causing the plane to ride roughly as it passes over. Another common type is caused by columns of heat rising from the ground due to the differing heat absorbency rates of ground areas. This causes the plane to rise and fall as it passes through them.

The most severe turbulence is found in thunderstorms. Pilots will not fly through a storm. At present there is no equipment that can detect simple turbulence. Turbulence can not usually be seen but an experienced pilot can tell where turbulence is likely to be encountered by reading cloud patterns and other atmospheric signs. When an area of turbulence is detected, pilots pass this on to other aircraft in the area as well as to their company, to warn other pilots.

Does the pilot try to avoid turbulence if possible? Why? Does it bother them as well?

Pilots will certainly not take off into an area of severe turbulence. There are several degrees of turbulence and, while a modern aircraft can withstand just about any degree of turbulence possible, it does create a very uncomfortable flight both for the passengers and the flight crew. "Besides," said one experienced captain, "it spills the coffee."

What is an air pocket?

There is really no such thing as an air pocket. What is sometimes described as an air pocket is simply turbulence. Occasionally, the plane will make a sudden drop in altitude giving the feeling that you are in a pocket without air to hold you up. This is not really the case and the term air pocket is not accurate.

How does the pilot get accurate weather information?

Before any flight, all pilots are provided with very complex and comprehensive weather reports. These are updated constantly during the flight. Pilots pass weather information back and forth constantly, to their companies, airports they pass over, and to other planes in the area. This keeps the weather information current and accurate.

Is it dangerous to fly through a thunderstorm?

Pilots do not fly through thunderstorms. They are very dangerous. A pilot will go to any lengths to avoid one. From the air, thunderstorms are visible for many miles in any direction and it is a simple manoeuvre to change course, which they do by a wide margin. Storms can be detected on radar and all aircraft will stay at least twenty miles away. If a storm is below a plane, the pilot must clear the top of the storm by at least five thousand feet.

What are wind-shears? How hazardous are they?

A wind shear occurs whenever the speed of the wind changes very rapidly in a very short space. For example, a change of 20 knots in wind speed occurring in a space of 1000 feet of altitude. This has the effect of making control of the aircraft very difficult. If it occurs at low levels, particularly while taking off or landing, it can be hazardous. Wind shears tend to occur at particular locations. Pilots are aware of the possibility of encountering wind shear at those places and will prepare for it. In addition, the presence of wind shear conditions is constantly monitored and pilots are warned to be on guard for it.

Does it make any difference to the flight if it rains, snows, or shines? Does the pilot take-off and land differently under different weather conditions?

The techniques of taking off and landing do not vary much, no matter what the weather. Any adjustments made usually involve safety precautions, such as using additional thrust to ensure maximum lift off, or lower thrust to avoid a bumpy landing. In bad weather, the pilot will rely more on his instruments than visual observation. Today's aircraft are so sophisticated that manual adjustments for weather are minimal.

What happens if an airport is closed due to fog or bad weather and a flight has to be re-routed? Who decides where the plane will go?

Every flight has at least one alternate airport for use should the original destination be closed. Fuel requirements are that a plane carry enough fuel to reach an alternate airport if necessary. The pilot makes the decision where to head for in the event of a closed airport.

Who decides when and if the airport should be closed due to snow, fog, etc., and who orders re-opening?

The airport manager has the sole authority for closing and re-opening the airport. He will close the airport whenever physical conditions are such that it can no longer function. This can be due to weather, labour problems, congestion, or a number of other reasons. Should there be planes in the air when an airport is closed, the pilots are informed of the conditions on the ground and they make the decision whether or not to land. Once a plane is in the air the decision of when and where to land rests solely with the pilot.

QUESTIONS ABOUT THE AIR TERMINAL AND SECURITY PROCEDURES

Throughout the airport there are Exit doors that say Emergency Exit only - alarm will sound if opened. In the event that someone had to get out of the airport in a hurry and used one of these doors, what would happen?

An audible alarm would sound as soon as the door was opened and the police would respond. Emergency doors must always be unlocked for safety reasons. They are monitored constantly by security and the police.

A very nervous flyer travelling alone would probably find it easier if he could be accompanied from the baggage check area to the plane and also from the plane to the baggage claim area on arrival. How would he arrange this?

This should be arranged with the airline agents when you first check in. Providing you allow enough time, you will find that most airlines will oblige and arrange for somebody to accompany you to the plane. For assistance on landing, speak to the flight attendant. Stay in your seat while the other passengers disembark and the flight attendant will then arrange for the airline agent who meets the plane to have you accompanied to the baggage area. You may even find that the flight attendant, if leaving the plane immediately, will accompany you themselves.

It's embarrassing if the alarm is activated as I walk through the security check. What is most likely to start it off? Do they catch many people carrying weapons?

The walk-through security equipment is set to detect a

certain mass of metal and must be set no higher than a standard prescribed by Transport Canada and the airlines. In most cases the equipment is set well below that standard, so that almost any metal object might set off an alarm. Three coins might do it as well as keys, belt buckles and even some articles of clothing, like a bra that may contain metal parts. If the alarm sounds, the passenger is asked to step aside and be wanded by a hand-held device. If it detects a metal object the passenger will be asked to show what it is. If it becomes absolutely necessary, a passenger can be searched.

Some medically required objects like certain prostheses, or metal plates or screws implanted in a person's body, even shrapnel from old war wounds, will set off the alarm. If you have such objects in your body you should be prepared for this. In such cases, presentation of a medical certificate is not usually acceptable. You may be asked to show your prosthesis, or a scar or some other proof of medically implanted metal objects. This may seem unnecessarily harsh, but it has been known for terrorists to attempt to smuggle weapons on board hidden inside their bodies.

Under what circumstances would a passenger be refused entry to the security area?

Entry to the security area may be refused to any passenger considered to be unruly or intoxicated to a degree considered a danger to themselves or other people, or a passenger who refuses to surrender a dangerous object and one who, in the judgement of the security personnel, might be considered to pose a potential danger.

What do the security people look for on their X-ray equipment?

When passengers put their hand luggage on the conveyor belt, it goes through an X-ray scanner and all the contents of the bags can be seen by the security personnel on a screen. Any potentially dangerous objects such as knives, guns, ammunition, knitting needles, darts, aerosol cans, or anything that could cause an explosion, would be removed. If a passenger is returning to the point of take-off, and providing the removed article is not essential for travel, the passenger would be asked to leave it and claim it on their return. If the article is essential, or the passenger is not returning to that point, providing it is not a dangerous article such as a gun or a knife, the carrier will place it in a special box, carried in an inaccessible part of the aircraft.

What about certain religious orders that require their members to carry a ceremonial dagger?

The Civil Aviation Association recommend that any pointed object four inches or longer be confiscated before boarding a plane. Some religious orders require the wearing of a ceremonial dagger and if this is longer than the prescribed four inches, it will be removed and held for the passenger at their destination. Some religious sects also allow the wearing of a lapel pin in lieu of the actual dagger. These would be allowed.

Are there any items that I should not put through the X-ray equipment, such as film or computer disks?

Generally, anything being exposed to X-rays can be examined by the security people manually, if you request it. However the X-rays used in airport security equipment are very mild and most things can go through the equipment without fear of damage. Photographic film rated below 600 ASA, which is virtually any type of film except that used by professional photographers, can go through without danger, as can computer disks, either clean or with data stored on them. If you are in any doubt by all means ask the security people to examine them manually. Any electronic equipment, like a portable computer, a tape recorder or even a radio must be operational and will be tested to make sure that it does work. If the item can be easily opened, it will probably be inspected. If it doesn't work, or is not what it seems to be, it simply will not be allowed to go on the plane.

If someone jokingly uses the words highjack, bombs, or something similar, what is likely to happen?

Highjacking, terrorism, bombs, are all extremely serious concerns, not only to air passengers but to the airlines and airport personnel as well. Whenever anybody is heard to use these words, whether in jest or not, it will be taken very seriously and there are severe penalties for this kind of irresponsible behaviour. You will see warning signs posted throughout the airport. When it happens, the security personnel will immediately call in the police. The security guard is not required to determine whether or not the person was joking. It will be assumed that they were serious. The person is almost always charged and would almost certainly not be allowed to board their flight.

Should this happen during a flight, the captain would be informed and he would immediately advise the police of the incident. If the captain believes the threat to be serious, he may land at the nearest airport and the plane would be met by the police. The passenger who made the remarks would be escorted off for questioning. Such things are simply not funny and the airlines, police and airport security cannot afford to take any chances.

If I should get restless in the passenger's lounge, can I leave the holding area and come back through again later? How many times can I do this?

You can leave the holding area and come and go as often as you wish. You will have to go through security each time that you re-enter the holding area. Remember that the responsibility for catching your plane is yours. Pre-boarding is usually about fifteen minutes before departure and there is no reason why you shouldn't be able to stay outside right up to the final boarding announcement.

Where can I get a plan of airports to help me find my way in a new situation?

Most travel agents and all airlines have plans of all major airports in the U. S., Canada and the rest of the world, which they will be able to show you. You can also find plans of major airports in some airline magazines found in the seat pockets of the plane.

Which are the busiest air terminals?

Pilots classify an airport as busier than another in relation to the total traffic in the area and not just the number of takeoffs and landings that take place there. For example, Vancouver is considered very busy because of the mountains and ocean in the vicinity which tends to compress all air traffic into a small area. Other cities have perhaps more than one major airport, such as London, Paris and New York, making more traffic to be contended with.

In general, the busiest in Canada are Toronto, Montreal and Vancouver. In North America, Chicago, New York and Atlanta; and in the world, London, Amsterdam, Athens, Paris and Hong Kong.

QUESTIONS ABOUT HEALTH CONCERNS OF THE TRAVELLER

Are there some physical conditions with which a person should definitely not fly?

There are some conditions under which a person should not attempt to fly. Some of them are: certain heart conditions, any serious lung condition, especially one that may require the use of oxygen, and uncontrolled hypertension. It is not advisable to fly with an ear infection, or any ear condition which may cause an inability to equalize pressure. Many doctors do not recommend flying with a bad cold or the flu.

It is not dangerous, either to the mother or the baby, to fly while pregnant. However, most airlines have rules for pregnant passengers to avoid the possibility of dealing with a birth while in the air. They will usually permit a pregnant woman to fly providing she has more than six weeks before normal delivery is expected.

What happens if someone is taken ill on a flight or a baby is born?

Should a passenger be taken ill during a flight, the flight attendants would first call for any doctor or nurse on board to come forward to assist. The captain would be notified and, depending on the seriousness of the passenger's condition, he may decide to make an unscheduled landing at the nearest available airport.

Should a pregnant woman appear to be going into labour, the same procedure would be followed. If there is a doctor or a nurse on board who is willing to help, the baby could probably be delivered on board. If the mother and the baby appear to be strong and healthy, the pilot would probably continue on to the flight's destination unless there were complications that would require immediate hospitalization.

Pregnant mothers present something of a problem for the airline. They cannot legally deny boarding to a pregnant woman but they prefer not to if she is past her seventh month. It is a good idea, if you are in this condition, to carry a letter from your physician stating how far along you are and that you are in good health and free from known complications relating to your pregnancy.

What causes air sickness?

Air sickness, sea-sickness or car-sickness is really just motion sickness. It is thought to be caused by excessive stimulation in the receptors of the inner ear by the motion of the vehicle. Alternatively, it may be caused by your confused brain as what your eyes see differs from information coming in from other parts of your body notably, the equilibrium receptors in your inner ear. This can occur when a plane is banking. Your eyes tell your brain that you are leaning sideways to the ground, which in fact you are, but other receptors tell it that you are still sitting upright.

Air sickness does not occur very often. People becoming sick on a plane are more often ill from some other cause than just the effect of flying. When it does occur, it is more likely to be on a long flight when the passenger is fatigued or didn't eat properly prior to boarding. It can also occur when a flight goes through a number of altitude changes to which some people have difficulty adjusting.

An effective, natural remedy for motion sickness is ginger, either in candied form or in ginger supplement capsules available at a health-food store. There are also compact electronic devices available to be worn on your wrist that are said to interrupt signals from your brain to your stomach. These may alleviate the problem.

Sometimes, motion sickness, either real or anticipated, becomes, in itself, a reason not to fly. In this case the thought of vomiting, especially in public, can become a phobia of its own.

Why do my ears hurt when the plane descends? What can I do about it - sucking a candy or chewing gum doesn't seem to help. Does everyone experience pain in the ears?

Your ears hurt because of the change in pressure. The pressure inside your ear is different to that outside. It will not burst or damage anything in your ear. By sucking or chewing you are trying to open the eustachian tube to allow the higher pressure to escape thus equalizing the pressure within your ears. The most effective way of doing this is to pinch your nostrils together and blow out gently but firmly. Swallowing may also help, or simulating a yawn by relaxing and stretching the muscles at the back of your mouth and throat. Not everybody experiences this pain. Frequent flyers, like pilots or flight attendants, become so accustomed to the changing pressures that their bodies adjust automatically. Some people simply don't notice or adjust very quickly. Unless there is some problem in your ear, like an infection or a blockage of the canals, the problem is temporary and not dangerous. It is best to check with your doctor before flying if this is a problem for you.

Sometimes when we are taking off the air pressure seems to make my stomach feel bloated and uncomfortable. Why is this?

There is always a certain amount of air inside your body. It collects in pockets wherever there is space for it. The largest such space in your body is the abdominal cavity. When the pressure in the plane changes, as on ascent or descent, this trapped air has to adjust to the increased or decreased pressure outside your body. For the few seconds or so that it takes to equalize this pressure you can feel bloated and uncomfortable.

If I am travelling with a child or an adult, and they contract a childhood disease or some other infectious condition, should I allow them to fly? Would it be prohibited?

Anybody with a contagious or infectious disease should not fly. In fact, the airlines, if they know of it, will not allow the person to fly. Flight attendants are instructed to watch for any signs of such a problem and a person suspected of having a disease will be asked to leave the plane.

Is it advisable to drink lots of fluids while flying?

The air in a plane tends to be very dry and most people become dehydrated especially on long trips. It is important to replenish the body fluids by drinking as much liquid as you can throughout your flight. Alcohol is dehydrating and is best avoided. Tea, coffee, colas and many other soft drinks contain caffeine which acts as a diuretic adding to the loss of fluid rather than helping it. The best liquid to drink is, simply, water.

What effect does alcohol have on the system when in the air

The effects of alcohol are doubled while at higher altitudes because of the limited oxygen in the plane's atmosphere. A rule of thumb is that one drink in the air is equal to two on the ground, both in its intoxicating effects and in its effect on your bladder and other organs.

Sometimes fearful flyers will consume large amounts of alcohol or tranquillizers prior to or during a flight, but find that it has little effect on them until they step off the plane. Why is this?

When a person is anxious, their body secretes adrenaline to give them the energy needed to counteract their fear. A fearful flyer's adrenaline secretions are already in overdrive and this can actually counteract the effects of the tranquillizer and/or the alcohol. Once on the ground again, the adrenaline flow returns to normal and the effects of the drugs kick in.

Can I take prescription drugs into other countries? Do I need a letter from my doctor?

You can take a reasonable supply of normal medications, whether prescription or over-the-counter, into most foreign countries, but you may be required to show why you are carrying them. This is particularly important for such drugs as tranquillizers or narcotics, but it applies equally to any drug, even comparatively harmless ones like Aspirin or cold medications. For this reason it is advisable to carry a letter from your doctor outlining your condition. In addition, carry a copy of the actual prescription. Make sure it shows the name and address of your doctor as well as the medication prescribed. If you require your medication regularly, remember to take along an extra supply in case your return is delayed.

In order to obtain more medication in a strange place, you will probably have to obtain another prescription from a local doctor and this can be difficult in a foreign country. If there is an embassy or consulate where you are, they would probably be able to recommend a doctor for you, as would your hotel. However, medical standards in some countries are sometimes strange and often inferior to those we are used to at home. The International Association for Medical Assistance to Travellers, (I.A.M.A.T.) publishes a directory of doctors and medical facilities around the world able to provide care consistent with North American standards and in our own language. The directory can be obtained for a donation, by writing to: I.A.M.A.T., 40 Regal Road, Guelph, Ontario, N1K 1B5, Canada. Other things to remember are:

• carry documentation concerning any allergies, particularly allergies to drugs.

• take along a copy of the prescription for your glasses or contact lenses. Many a holiday has been ruined when glasses have been lost or broken.

How do I know what vaccinations and immunizations are required for travellers going to other countries and where do I get them?

The public health department of your local city should be able to give you this information, or at least tell you where to get it. Travel agents and many doctors also have lists of vaccination requirements of the most commonly visited countries. As well, the International Association for Medical Assistance to Travellers (I.A.M.A.T.) publishes a complete directory of required and recommended vaccinations for every country in the world. This directory also gives information on the safety of the water, availability of medical care and other pertinent health information for various countries.

Can a person die of fright?

No. Death from fright alone is an extremely rare event. In fact, it is doubtful if anyone has ever died just from being frightened. People who were said to have died of fright really died as the result of other bodily malfunctions, which may or may not have been triggered by the frightening experience.

GENERAL QUESTIONS ABOUT TRAVEL

What are the busiest travel times in the year?

Christmas is regarded as the busiest period for travel closely followed by Thanksgiving in the United States. No matter where you may be going, look for crowded airports and flights, delays and slow service. Also look for the highest prices at this time of the year.

Next - any other holiday. Remember to check for holidays in other countries that may differ from our own. You may leave Canada in relative calm, only to arrive on a major holiday weekend overseas.

Summer is busy all the time, especially in major tourist areas like Europe. Similarly, you can expect busy travel in any warm place, such as the Caribbean or Mexico, during our winter, or during special events like the Quebec Winter Carnival, the New Orleans Mardi Gras or the Olympic Games.

Before travelling, you or your travel agent should check for such things as conventions, conferences or other events that may make for crowded facilities and busy travel at your destination.

What's the difference between First Class, Business Class and Economy Class? Does it vary between Domestic and Overseas flights?

This varies from airline to airline but generally speaking, First Class means that you are seated in the front of the plane, in wider, more comfortable seats with more space around you. The food and service are better and more luxurious, with any number of frills like menus, individually served meals, slippers, free champagne before take-off, special priority baggage handling and so on. Business Class is similar to First Class, but is geared more to the business traveller, with special check-in and boarding, newspapers, special meals, wider seating, even telephone and fax service on some flights.

Economy Class passengers are usually seated in the rear of the plane. They receive standard meals and somewhat less luxurious seating. While economy class service on most airlines is still very good, there may be less of it. The same class differences apply on domestic and overseas flights, except that often the service on overseas flights is more geared to the destination - like food from the region you are going to and so on.

First Class is no longer available on airlines in Canada.

What is the difference between a Regular fare, an Advance Booking fare and a Charter? What is the difference in service?

A regular fare is simply a ticket for a scheduled flight on an airline, for which you have paid full fare. You can book your flight in advance, or just prior to boarding the aircraft. You can change your flight to any other flight without extra charge. Usually, regular fare tickets are fully refundable, even after the flight, if you haven't used the ticket.

Advance booking fare is a ticket on a scheduled flight, which must be booked and sometimes paid for in advance of the flight. The exact timing depends on the requirements of the airline. Advance booking tickets are cheaper but not usually refundable. If they are, penalties are withheld. Depending on the offer, it may or may not be possible to change your flight and, most likely a penalty will be applied.

A Charter is a flight operated by an independent operator. They usually use aircraft of the regular airlines, although some do have their own. The important difference is that, with a Charter flight, you are dealing not with the airline but with the charter operator. If anything goes wrong with the flight arrangements or, if as sometimes happens, the charter flight is cancelled, you must look to the charter operator for reimbursement rather than the airline.

In general, the service provided by the airlines or the charter operators is the same regardless of the type of fare paid. The only difference in service would depend on the class of fare, that is, First Class, Business Class or Economy.

What's the difference between a direct flight, a non-stop flight and a connecting flight?

A Direct flight means that your plane will go from point A to point B, but you may stop at one or several places in between.

A Non-stop flight means just that. You will go from point A to point B with no stops in between.

A Connecting flight means that you will have to change planes somewhere along your route.

I prefer certain seats in an aircraft. Can I book the seat I prefer in advance? What if I have to change planes and airlines? Can I make a guaranteed reservation? Do you have seating plans for all types of aircraft?

Usually, you can book a preferred seat in advance. Simply request it at your travel agent or the airline office where you purchase your ticket. Most travel agents will have seating plans for the various types of aircraft available and can help you choose the seat you would prefer. The seating configuration within identical planes may differ from airline to airline, so a specific seat in the plane of one airline might not be available on another.

You can make a guaranteed reservation, but this will depend on the class of travel you are purchasing. Your travel agent will be able to advise you.

How can I arrange to be pre-boarded?

Pre-boarding means that certain passengers, usually elderly people, handicapped people or those travelling with small children, are allowed to board the plane ahead of the other passengers. If, for any reason, you require to be pre-boarded this should be discussed with the agent at the departure gate or when purchasing your ticket. Unless there is an obvious reason for pre-boarding, you will probably be asked to give your reasons for the request. Pre-boarding is not simply a service available for the asking. Rather, it is done to get passengers who may be slower, or who have difficulty getting into their seats, on first and so speed up the boarding of the others. A nervous flyer should make this fact known to the agent and, if pre-boarding would help, they would be accommodated.

Physically handicapped passengers should notify the airline agent of that fact at the time of purchasing their ticket and most certainly at the time of checking in. This is most important, as airlines must limit the number of physically handicapped passengers on any one flight for reasons of safety. It is possible that an airline may refuse to carry a handicapped person who arrives without prior notification, simply because they already had more than their allowable limit on the flight.

What happens if I lose my ticket before I leave on my trip?

Loss of your ticket is not necessarily the loss of your trip. Most tickets can be replaced, under differing conditions depending on the type and class of travel you have purchased. The important thing to remember is that replacement of a lost ticket takes time. If there is not sufficient time to obtain the replacement before you are scheduled to fly, then you will probably have to purchase a new ticket and arrange for the old one to be refunded later.

Any unused full-price ticket (i.e. First Class, Business Class or Economy Class), is refundable, even after the date of the flight. Other types of ticket (such as Advanced Booking, Seat Sales and so on), may or may not be refundable, or there may be penalties charged in the event of a refund or replacement. Most airlines will replace a lost ticket, providing that no one has used it. Unfortunately, if that happens, you will be out of luck. If you lose your ticket, notify the airline or your travel agent immediately to prevent someone else from using it.

What happens if I lose my return ticket?

Basically the procedure is the same as for a lost ticket, except that there almost certainly would not be time to obtain a replacement ticket before the time that you wanted to return. You will have to purchase a new ticket in order to get home and this would be subject to availability of seats at the time. You may not be able to fly back on the same flight that you had originally booked. Once you get home you should get in touch with the airline or your travel agent, who will arrange for refund of your lost ticket. This may take some time to complete, perhaps several months.

Another thing to remember, should you have to purchase another return ticket, you will have to pay the full regular one-way fare applicable at that time, which can cost more than you paid for the original return ticket. Most certainly, it will cost more than one half of the return fare. It doesn't pay to lose your ticket!

What happens if I miss my plane?

This depends on the class of service you have purchased. If you have paid regular fare (First Class, Business Class or Economy) and you miss your plane, you will simply have to go to the airline or travel agent and re-book on the next available flight. Alternatively, you can cash in your ticket for a refund if you decide not to go. For other types of tickets (Excursion, Advanced Booking or Seat Sales), rebooking you on another flight will be at the airline's discretion, subject to availability of seats on other flights. If you do miss your flight, the best thing to do is go to the airline counter and explain what has happened. Providing they have seats available they will probably re-book you on another flight. If they won't, then you will have to purchase another ticket at regular fare.

It does sometimes happen that airlines will adjust their schedules after your ticket has been issued and the times and dates shown on your ticket may not then be correct. When this happens, the airlines will attempt to notify you or your travel agent, who is then supposed to notify you of the change. If they fail to do so, or can't reach you for some reason, then you may arrive at the airport at the correct date and time only to find that your flight has left, or is not due to leave until next week, or has been cancelled altogether. As a precaution, always confirm your flight time with the airline or travel agent at least seventy-two hours prior to the date and time shown on your ticket.

Is it wise to have insurance when travelling?

It is probably a good idea to carry insurance, especially if you are going overseas. Insurance is available for all kinds of risks, from lost luggage to major medical expenses. Your travel agent can give you details of what is available and the cost, which is usually quite reasonable. Certainly, you should purchase health insurance if you are going to another country, especially when travelling to the United States, where an unexpected medical problem could leave you having to pay a large bill. Even countries with national health plans, like Great Britain, do not cover visitors to their country and medical expenses can be quite substantial. Cancellation insurance can be purchased which covers the cost of a return flight, should it be necessary for you to return home earlier in an emergency, or should you be unable to make the original return flight for similar reasons.

What is the procedure to collect on the insurance if I can't fly for health reasons?

Usually, your cancellation insurance will cover any non-refundable portion of your ticket. The procedure for claiming will differ from company to company but, basically, it will involve completing a claim form, obtaining a medical certificate or other evidence to support your claim, obtaining whatever refund you can from the airline, and then claiming the difference from the insurance company. Your travel agent who sold you the insurance will have details and will probably handle the claim for you.

When travelling to the United States, sometimes the immigration check is at the point of departure and sometimes at the destination. Why is this?

The United States maintains Customs and Immigration

offices in some of the larger foreign airports, to provide immigration clearance to travellers going to the United States. Whether you clear immigration before leaving the foreign country or on arrival in the U.S. really depends on where you are going. If you are travelling to a large centre, like New York or Los Angeles the chances are that you would go through immigration there, rather than overseas because the larger centres have adequate facilities for handling large numbers of people coming in. If you are travelling to a smaller centre like Las Vegas, which does not have a lot of international flights coming in, you would probably clear immigration before you leave. If you are travelling from a Canadian airport that does not have United States Customs and Immigration officers stationed there, you would go through Immigration on arrival at your destination.

When do I need a visa?

A visa is really permission from a foreign country for the holder to enter that country. It may take the form of just a rubber stamp in your passport, or it may be a separate document with your picture on it. Whether you require a visa or not depends on the country or countries you will be visiting. Some countries require them, some don't. Some countries issue visas when you enter the country, others require you to apply in advance from your home country.

In order to be safe, be sure that your travel agent knows exactly where you intend to go on your trip. If you are going to London and while there you decide to visit Hungary for a weekend, you will require a Hungarian visa. You will soon find you should have applied back home, well in advance.

Requirements for visas change frequently and depend on your citizenship. You should never assume that a visa is not required. Check with your travel agent.

When do I need a passport?

You should carry your passport whenever you leave the country, whether you are going around the world or just over the border. More and more frequently, immigration officials in the United States now require a passport for admission.

Your passport is not just a border crossing document. It is the best identification document you can have. In some countries you must show your passport in order to register in a hotel. Some hotels may require you to surrender your passport when you check in. It can also be used as identification for cashing travellers cheques, using credit cards or when seeking assistance at embassies or consulates overseas.

It is a very good idea to make two copies of the page in your passport that contains the passport number and your name and personal details. Carry one on your person, separate from the actual passport. Leave the other at home as a backup with a dependable person. Should you lose your passport, having the number and information readily available will save a lot of time in obtaining a replacement through the local High Commission, Embassy or Consulate. Your passport is an extremely valuable document. Treat it with respect and pride. Don't leave home without it!

BON VOYAGE

AND

HAPPY LANDINGS!